Oracle Business Intelligence: The Condensed Guide to Analysis and Reporting

A fast track guide to uncovering the analytical power of Oracle Business Intelligence: Analytic SQL, Oracle Discoverer, Oracle Reports, and Oracle Warehouse Builder

Yuli Vasiliev

PUBLISHING

BIRMINGHAM - MUMBAI

Oracle Business Intelligence: The Condensed Guide to Analysis and Reporting

First published: October 2010

Production Reference: 1071010

Published by Packt Publishing Ltd.
32 Lincoln Road
Olton
Birmingham, B27 6PA, UK.

ISBN 978-1-849681-18-6

www.packtpub.com

Cover Image by Sandeep Babu (sandyjb@gmail.com)

Credits

Author
Yuli Vasiliev

Reviewers
Ivan Brigida

Hans Forbrich

Peter McLarty

Acquisition Editor
Stephanie Moss

Development Editor
Reshma Sundareshan

Technical Editors
Neha Damle

Manjeet Kaur Saini

Indexer
Monica Ajmera Mehta

Editorial Team Leader
Gagandeep Singh

Project Team Leader
Lata Basantani

Project Coordinator
Shubhanjan Chatterjee

Proofreader
Chris Smith

Graphics
Geetanjali Sawant

Production Coordinator
Shantanu Zagade

Cover Work
Shantanu Zagade

About the Author

Yuli Vasiliev is a software developer, freelance author, and consultant currently specializing in open source development, databases, Business Intelligence (BI), Java technologies, and service-oriented architecture (SOA). He has over 12 years' experience using Oracle products and is the author of *PHP Oracle Web Development* (*Packt Publishing*, 2007), as well as several other books.

About the Reviewers

Ivan Brigida completed his M.A. in Applied Mathematics and Cybernetics at the Moscow State University (2008), where he specialized in the Software Engineering field. He worked for 3 years as a test engineer of a Computer Aided Software Engineering tool, which is now an IBM product. In 2010, he finished M.A. in Economics at the New Economic School, specialized in data analysis (econometrics) and finance fields. Now he is working in the largest commercial bank in Russia (Sberbank), one of the top twenty world banks on capitalization. He is doing analysis of business data, where he develops and implements financial models for the Management Information System of the bank.

His hobbies include playing volleyball, reading books, and theatre.

I am grateful to my mother, who supported and believed in me all these years. Also, I would like to thank my classmates Alexey Sapozhnikov and Sergey Slizko, who participated in the brilliant discussions on the sleepless nights and gave a lot of interesting ideas and insights.

Hans Forbrich is a well-known consultant and trainer of Oracle technologies including Database Server, Application Server, Fusion Middleware, and Oracle BI products. He started with Oracle database in 1984, after having used and evaluated quite a few other database technologies, and has been encouraging people to fully leverage their Oracle investment ever since.

For *Packt Publishing*, Hans has been a technical reviewer for a number of Oracle titles such as *Mastering Oracle Scheduler in Oracle 11g Databases* and *Middleware Management with Oracle Enterprise Manager Grid Control 10g R5*.

Hans is an Oracle ACE Director (`http://www.oracle.com/technetwork/community/oracle-ace/index.html`), and is frequently invited to give talks about Oracle technology around the world. He is the owner and principal consultant of Forbrich Computer Consulting Ltd., which specializes in architecture, planning, and technology training in Canada and the United States.

In his other life, Hans is a supporter of the arts community and is actively involved with the Edmonton Opera as a sponsor, contributor, and chorister.

> I'd like to thank my wife Susanne and all my 'children' (who are grown up now) for their patience and understanding as I disappear into the Oracle tech world for long periods of time.

Peter McLarty is a Senior Consultant working in Brisbane Australia. Peter has worked with technology all his life. He is presently employed by Pacific DBMS Pty Ltd.

He works with Oracle database, Middleware Fusion, and Enterprise Manager with clients in Brisbane. Peter's career spans 25 years of technology and 13 years in database management.

Peter has worked mainly in Australia and Asia. Peter's other interests include studying Asia and its cultures and of course its food, sailing, and football. He can be found supporting his team each season at the stadium.

Peter has also been a reviewer of *Middleware Management with Oracle Enterprise Manager 10gR5* and *Oracle 10g/11g Data and Database Management Utilities* (*Packt Publishing*).

He has a wife and two children who say they have to suffer through the times of editing books amongst other projects. Peter would like to thank them for their understanding and allowing dad to do his stuff at times.

Table of Contents

Preface

While often used interchangeably, data and information do not mean the same thing. In a few simple words, data is what you can save, transform, or retrieve, whereas information is what you normally use in a decision-making process. On the other hand, these two terms are very closely related, as information is taken out of data. And sometimes, it may be quite sufficient to take a glance at your data by issuing a simple query, obtaining the required information, and getting your question answered.

Having data, though, does not automatically mean having information. In general terms, obtaining information is a process of transforming data. Depending on the information you need, the process of extracting information from data may be as simple as issuing a simple SQL query against it, or may be complex enough that it requires you to issue a great deal of complicated analytical queries against data stored in different sources, and in different formats.

SQL, which has been the primary tool for extracting information from data for decades, hits its ceiling when it comes to answering business analysis questions. The problem is not only in that it is sometimes too hard to write SQL statements that reflect required business functionality, but also that SQL is designed to work only with structured data stored in a relational database, while you may need to access unstructured or semi-structured data.

The limitations of SQL pushed some vendors to come up with **BI** (**Business Intelligence**) tools, which simplify the process of analyzing and publishing business data stored in both a database and external sources, thus enabling better decision-making. Using BI tools, you can easily prepare your data, wherever it is found, for analysis and reporting, thus creating and maintaining a business-oriented view of it.

This book introduces **Oracle Business Intelligence**, a suite of high-end tools from Oracle, which provide an effective means of delivering information, analysis, and efficiencies. You will learn how to use these powerful tools to your advantage when it comes to accessing the data that's available from a number of different sources and extracting the information you need to run your business.

What this book covers

As mentioned earlier, the book introduces the Oracle Business Intelligence platform, providing a suite of examples to help illustrate some key concepts. Here's a synopsis of what you will find in the book:

Chapter 1, Getting Business Information from Data, explains the concepts behind getting business information from data, giving you a basic understanding of what you need to answer your business questions promptly and efficiently.

Chapter 2, Introducing Oracle Business Intelligence, gives a comprehensive overview of the components included in the Oracle Business Intelligence package, as well as the Oracle Business Intelligence Tools package. It also explains how to install these packages on your machine. Although the installation process is given for Windows, it's similar for the other operating systems on which you might install this software.

Chapter 3, Working with Database Data, describes how to access and analyze data extracted from various sources, including Oracle Database and external source systems. You'll learn how to access and analyze relational data, leveraging the Business Intelligence features of Oracle Database as well as its computational power.

Chapter 4, Analyzing Data and Creating Reports, demonstrates the use of Oracle Business Intelligence components to analyze data and create reports, processing information that comes from the data you collect during business transactions. In particular, you'll look at Oracle Reports, Oracle BI Discoverer Plus, and Oracle BI Spreadsheet Add-In.

Chapter 5, Warehousing for Analysis and Reporting, explains the role of data warehousing for analysis and reporting, discussing how to build and use a Data Warehouse in an Oracle database. The chapter examples illustrate how you can integrate data from different transactional systems, facilitating business analysis with warehousing.

Chapter 6, Pivoting Through Data, discusses the use of pivoting to arrange data for effective analysis. You will look at how to change the layout or contents of an Oracle BI Discoverer Plus report, taking advantage of the *slice and dice* capability.

Chapter 7, Drilling Data Up and Down, gives the details on how to drill data up and down, navigating Discoverer worksheet data. In particular, you will learn how to use interactive reports, drilling into data for more detail.

Chapter 8, Advanced Analysis and Reporting, gives a comprehensive overview of the advanced analysis and reporting features of the Oracle Business Intelligence Discoverer Plus, explaining how to use Discoverer parameters, conditional formatting, and how to filter out data with conditions.

What you need for this book

The examples discussed in this book assume that you will be using the Oracle Discoverer tools, Oracle Reports Services, and Oracle Spreadsheet Add-In. Therefore, to follow the book's examples, you need to have the Oracle Business Intelligence suite as well as the Oracle Business Intelligence Tools suite installed on your computer. These products are part of Oracle Application Server 10g Release 2. Alternatively, you might use the Portal, Forms, Reports, and Discoverer suite, which is part of Oracle Fusion Middleware 11g R1. Whatever option you choose, though, you must also have access to an Oracle database 10g or 11g.

Like many Oracle products, all the earlier software can be obtained from the **Oracle Technology Network (OTN)** website and used for free under a development license, which allows for unlimited evaluation time. Later, if required, you can always buy products with full-use licenses.

Most Oracle products, including those that are mentioned earlier (and which you need to have installed to follow the sample code) are available for all major operating system platforms. Therefore you may be a Windows, Linux, or Solaris user, and still be able to install this software. For more details, refer to the appropriate document describing all the available platforms for individual products. You can find a link to such a document on each product's download page.

Who this book is for

This book is written for all those who want to learn how to use the Oracle Business Intelligence platform for analysis and reporting, including analysts, report builders, DBAs, and application developers.

A prerequisite for this book is a cursory understanding of the basic principles in the area of storing and retrieving business data with a RDBMS. However, you don't need to be a database guru to start using Oracle Business Intelligence tools to produce meaningful information from data. In this book, new and casual users are provided with detailed instructions on how to quickly get started with the Oracle Database Business Intelligence features, as well as the key components of the Oracle Business Intelligence suite, putting this handy software to immediate and productive use.

Conventions

In this book, you will find a number of styles of text that distinguish between different kinds of information. Here are some examples of these styles, and an explanation of their meaning.

Code words in text are shown as follows: "We can include other contexts through the use of the include directive."

A block of code is set as follows:

```
SELECT count(*) FROM employees WHERE (EXTRACT(YEAR FROM (SYSDATE))
                        - EXTRACT(YEAR FROM (hire_date))) >= 15;
```

When we wish to draw your attention to a particular part of a code block, the relevant lines or items are set in bold:

```
INSERT INTO salespersons VALUES ('violet', 'Violet Robinson');
INSERT INTO salespersons VALUES ('maya', 'Maya Silver');
INSERT INTO regions VALUES ('NA', 'North America');
INSERT INTO regions VALUES ('EU', 'Europe');
```

Any command-line input or output is written as follows:

```
start c:\oracle\product\11.2.0\dbhome_1\owb\UnifiedRepos\cat_owb.sql
```

New terms and **important words** are shown in bold. Words that you see on the screen, in menus or dialog boxes for example, appear in the text like this: "clicking the **Next** button moves you to the next screen".

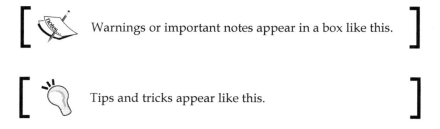

Warnings or important notes appear in a box like this.

Tips and tricks appear like this.

Reader feedback

Feedback from our readers is always welcome. Let us know what you think about this book—what you liked or may have disliked. Reader feedback is important for us to develop titles that you really get the most out of.

To send us general feedback, simply send an e-mail to feedback@packtpub.com, and mention the book title via the subject of your message.

If there is a book that you need and would like to see us publish, please send us a note in the **SUGGEST A TITLE** form on www.packtpub.com or e-mail suggest@packtpub.com.

If there is a topic that you have expertise in and you are interested in either writing or contributing to a book, see our author guide on www.packtpub.com/authors.

Customer support

Now that you are the proud owner of a Packt book, we have a number of things to help you to get the most from your purchase.

Downloading the example code for this book

You can download the example code files for all Packt books you have purchased from your account at http://www.PacktPub.com. If you purchased this book elsewhere, you can visit http://www.PacktPub.com/support and register to have the files e-mailed directly to you.

Errata

Although we have taken every care to ensure the accuracy of our content, mistakes do happen. If you find a mistake in one of our books—maybe a mistake in the text or the code—we would be grateful if you would report this to us. By doing so, you can save other readers from frustration and help us improve subsequent versions of this book. If you find any errata, please report them by visiting http://www.packtpub.com/support, selecting your book, clicking on the **let us know** link, and entering the details of your errata. Once your errata are verified, your submission will be accepted and the errata will be uploaded on our website, or added to any list of existing errata, under the Errata section of that title. Any existing errata can be viewed by selecting your title from http://www.packtpub.com/support.

Piracy

Piracy of copyright material on the Internet is an ongoing problem across all media. At Packt, we take the protection of our copyright and licenses very seriously. If you come across any illegal copies of our works, in any form, on the Internet, please provide us with the location address or website name immediately so that we can pursue a remedy.

Please contact us at `copyright@packtpub.com` with a link to the suspected pirated material.

We appreciate your help in protecting our authors, and our ability to bring you valuable content.

Questions

You can contact us at `questions@packtpub.com` if you are having a problem with any aspect of the book, and we will do our best to address it.

1
Getting Business Information from Data

Most businesses today use Business Intelligence (BI), the process of obtaining business information from available data, to control their affairs. If you're new to Business Intelligence, then this definition may leave you with the following questions:

- What is data?
- What is the information obtained from it?
- What is the difference between data and the information obtained from it?

You may be confused even more if you learn that data represents groups of information related to an object or a set of objects. Depending on your needs, though, such groups of information may or may not be immediately useful, and often require additional processing such as filtering, formatting, and/or calculating to take on a meaning.

For example, information about your customers may be organized in a way that is stored in several database tables related to each other. For security purposes, some pieces of information stored in this way may be encoded, or just represented in binary, and therefore not immediately readable. It's fairly obvious that some processing must be applied before you can make use of such information.

So, data can be thought of as the lowest level of abstraction from which meaningful information is derived. But what is information anyway? Well, a piece of information normally represents an answer to a certain question. For example, you want to know how many new customers have registered on your site this year. An answer to this question can be obtained with a certain query issued against the table containing customer registration dates, giving you the information you asked for.

In this introduction chapter, you'll look at the basic concepts behind Business Intelligence. Proceeding with the discussion on data and information, it then moves on to describe what business questions you might need to answer, and how to find those answers from the data available at your disposal.

Listed as short bullets, here are the main topics of the chapter:

- Basic introduction to data, information, and Business Intelligence
- Answering basic business questions
- Answering probing analytical questions
- Asking business questions using data access tool
- Deriving information from existing data
- Accessing transactional and dimensional data

Data, information, and Business Intelligence

As you just learned, although the terms **data** and **information** refer to similar things, they aren't really interchangeable as there is some difference in their meaning and spirit. Talking about data, as a rule, involves its structure, format, storage, as well as ways in which you can access and manipulate it. In contrast, when talking about information, you mean food for your decision-making process. So, data can be viewed as low-level information structures, where the internal representation matters. Therefore, the ways in which you can extract useful information from data entirely depend on the structure and storage of that data.

The following diagram gives a conceptual view of delivering information from different data sets:

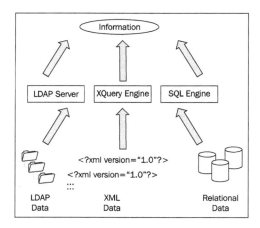

As you can see from the figure, information can be derived from different data sources, and by different means. Once it's derived, though, it doesn't matter where it has come from, letting its consumers concentrate on the business aspects rather than on the specifics of the internal structure. For example, you might derive some pieces of data from the Web, using the Oracle Database's XQuery feature, and then process it as native database data.

To produce meaningful information from your data, you will most likely need to perform several processing steps, load new data, and summarize the data. This is why the Business Intelligence layer usually sits on top of many data sources, consolidating information from various business systems and heterogeneous platforms.

The following figure gives a graphical depiction of a Business Intelligence system. In particular, it shows you that the Business Intelligence layer consumes information derived from various sources and heterogeneous platforms.

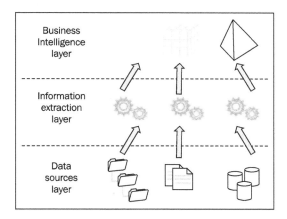

It is intuitively clear that the ability to solve problems is greatly enhanced if you can effectively handle all the information you're getting. On the other hand, extracting information from data coming in from different sources may become a nightmare if you try to do it on your own, with only the help of miscellaneous tools. Business Intelligence comes to the rescue here, ensuring that the extraction, transformation, and consolidation of data from disparate sources becomes totally transparent to you.

For example, when using a Business Intelligence application for reporting, you may never figure out exactly what happens behind the scenes when you instruct the system to prepare another report. The information you need for such a report may be collected from many different sources, hiding the complexities associated with handling heterogeneous data. But, without Business Intelligence, that would be a whole different story, of course. Imagine for a moment that you have to issue several queries against different systems, using different tools, and you then have to consolidate the results somehow—all just to answer a single business question such as: what are the top three customers for the preceding quarter?

As you have no doubt realized, the software at the Business Intelligence layer is used to provide a business-centric view of data, eliminating as much of the technology-specific logic as possible. What this means in practice is that information consumers working at the Business Intelligence layer may not even know that, say, customer records are stored in a **Lightweight Directory Access Protocol (LDAP)** database, but purchase orders are kept in a relational database.

The kind of business questions you may need to answer

As you just learned, Business Intelligence is here to consolidate information from disparate sources so that you need not concern yourself with it. Okay, but why might you need to gather and process heterogeneous data? The answer is clear. You might need it in order to answer analytical questions that allow you to understand and run your business better.

In the following two sections, you'll look at some common questions that Business Intelligence can help you answer. Then, you'll see how you can ask those questions with the help of Business Intelligence tools.

Answering basic business questions

The set of questions you may need your Business Intelligence system to answer will vary depending on your business and, of course, your corresponding functions. However, to give you a taste of what Business Intelligence can do for you, let's first look at some questions that are commonly brought up by business users:

- What is the average salary throughout the entire organization?
- Which customers produce the most revenue?
- What is the amount of revenue each salesman brought in over the preceding quarter?
- What is the profitability of each product?

If you run your business online, you may be also interested in hit counting and traffic analysis questions, such as the following:

- How much traffic does a certain account generate over a month?
- What pages in your site are most visited?
- What are the profits made online?

Looking at the business analysis requests presented here, a set of questions related to your own business may flash into your mind.

Answering probing analytical questions

In the preceding section, you looked at some common questions a business analyst is usually interested in asking. But bowing to the reality, you may have to answer more probing questions in your decision-making process, in order to determine changes in the business and find ways to improve it. Here are some probing analytical questions you might need to find answers to:

- How do sales for this quarter compare to sales for the preceding quarter?
- What factors impact our sales?
- Which products are sold better together?
- What are ten top-selling products in this region?
- What are the factors influencing the likelihood of purchase?

As you can see, each of these questions reflects a certain business problem. Looking through the previous list, though, you might notice that some of the questions shown here can be hard to formulate with the tools available in a computer application environment.

There's nothing to be done here; computers like specific questions. Unlike humans, machines can give you exactly what you ask for, not what you actually mean. So, even an advanced Business Intelligence application will require you to be as specific as possible when it comes to putting a question to it.

It's fairly clear that the question about finding the factors impacting sales needs to be rephrased to become understandable for a Business Intelligence application. How you would rephrase it depends on the specifics of your business, of course.

Often, it's good practice to break apart a problem into simpler questions. For example, the first question on the above list—the one about comparing quarter sales—might be logically divided into the following two questions:

- What are the sales figures for this quarter?
- What are the sales figures for the last quarter?

Once you get these questions answered, you can compare the results, thus answering the original, more generically phrased question. It can also provide one definition or variation for drill down.

In the above example, it's fairly obvious what specific questions can be derived from the generic question. There may be probing questions, though, whose derived questions are not so obvious. For example, consider the following question: What motivates a customer to buy? This could perhaps be broken down into the following questions:

- Where did visitors come from?
- Which pages did they visit before reaching the product page?

Of course, the above list does not seem to be complete—some other questions might be added.

Asking business questions using data-access tools

As you might guess, although all these questions sound simple when formulated in plain English, they are more difficult to describe when using data-access tools. If you're somewhat familiar with SQL, you might notice that most of the analytical questions discussed here cannot be easily expressed with the help of SQL statements, even if the underlying data is relational.

For example, the problem of finding the top three salespersons for a year may require you to write a multi-line SQL request including several sub-queries. Here is what such a query might look like:

```
SELECT emp.ename salesperson, top_emp_orders.sales sales
FROM
  (SELECT all_orders.sales_empno empno, all_orders.total_sales
   FROM
     (SELECT sales_empno, SUM(ord_total) total_sales, RANK() OVER
                           (ORDER BY SUM(ord_total) DESC) sal_rank
      FROM orders
      WHERE EXTRACT(YEAR FROM ord_dt) = 2009
```

```
       GROUP BY sales_empno
      )all_orders
     WHERE all_orders.sal_rank<=3
    )top_emp_orders, employees emp
  WHERE top_emp_orders.empno = emp.empno
  ORDER BY sales DESC;
```

This might produce something like this:

```
Oracle SQL*Plus                                    _ □ ×
 File  Edit  Search  Options  Help
  9        )all_orders
 10         WHERE all_orders.sal_rank<=3
 11        )top_emp_orders, employees emp
 12      WHERE top_emp_orders.empno = emp.empno
 13      ORDER BY sales DESC;

 SALESPERSON        SALES
 --------------- ----------
 Polonski           375965
 Petrov             348264
 Silver             324117

 SQL>
```

If you're not an SQL guru of course, writing the above query and then debugging it could easily take a couple of hours. Determining profitability by customer, for example, might take you another couple of hours to write a proper SQL query. In other words, business questions are often somewhat tricky (if possible at all) to implement with SQL.

All this does not mean that SQL is not used in the area of Business Intelligence. Quite the contrary, SQL is still indispensable here. In fact, SQL has a lot to offer when it comes to data analysis. *Chapter 3, Working with Database Data,* will provide a closer look at advanced SQL features you can use to summarize data over multiple tables. As you just saw, though, composing complex queries assumes solid SQL skills. Thankfully, most Business Intelligence tools use SQL behind the scenes totally transparently to users.

Now let's look at a simple example illustrating how you can get an analytical question answered with a Business Intelligence tool—Oracle BI Discoverer Plus in this particular example. Suppose you simply want to calculate the average salary sum over the organization. This example could use the records from the **hr.employees** demonstration table. Creating a worksheet representing the records of a database table in the Discoverer Plus will be discussed in detail later in *Chapter 4, Analyzing Data and Creating Reports*, which focuses on issues related to analyzing data, and creating reports with the tools available through the Oracle Business Intelligence suite. For now, look at the following screenshot to see what such a worksheet might look like:

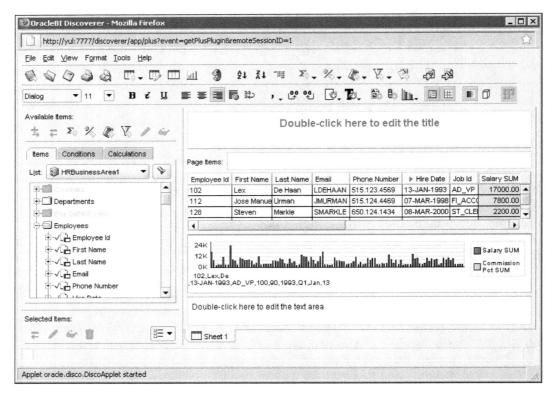

As you can see in the previous screenshot, a Discoverer Plus worksheet is similar to one in MS Excel. As in Excel, there are toolbars and menus offering a lot of options for manipulating and analyzing data presented on the worksheet. In addition, Discoverer Plus offers **Item Navigator**, which enables you to add data to (or remove it from) the worksheet. The data structure you can see in Item Navigator is retrieved from the database.

When we return to our example, answering the question: "what is the average salary across the organization?"Similarly, in Excel, it is as simple as selecting the **Salary SUM** column on the worksheet, choosing an appropriate menu, and setting some parameters in the dialog shown next. After you click the **OK** button in this dialog box, the calculated average will be added to the worksheet in the position specified. So, the `Total` dialog shown in the following screenshot provides an efficient means for automating the process of creating a total on a specified data column:

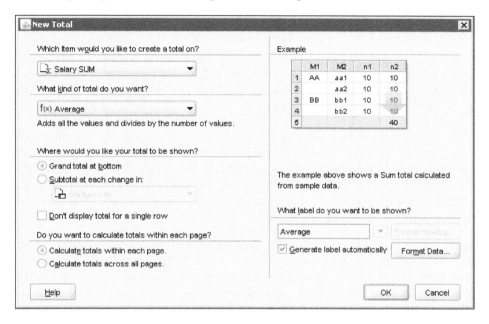

As you can see, this approach doesn't require you to write an SQL query on your own. Instead, Discoverer Plus will do it for you implicitly, thus allowing you to concentrate on business issues rather than data access issues.

This previous example should have given you a taste of what Business Intelligence can do for you. In the next chapters, you'll learn how you can make use of Business Intelligence applications to get these, and similar business questions, answered with a minimum of effort.

Deriving information from existing data

As you have no doubt realized, having data does not automatically mean having information. To turn data into meaningful information, analysis tools are required. Such tools can be implemented as standalone applications, or be integrated within a database or application server layer.

If you're dealing with data stored in a database, implementing data processing logic at the database tier seems to be most efficient. For example, Oracle Database offers a number of native features focusing on data analysis—the process of converting data into information. Sometimes, though, to obtain the required piece of information from your data, it's quite enough to issue a simple SQL query against it. For example, if you want to know the number of orders placed over a certain period of time, say, a year, this query might be as simple as the following:

```
SELECT count(*) FROM orders
WHERE EXTRACT(YEAR FROM ord_dt) = 2004
```

That is it. As you can see, the required piece of information is derived here from a relational table with a two-line SQL query. It's fairly obvious that you don't need any Business Intelligence tools to answer simple questions like the one in the previous example—SQL alone will be enough.

Unfortunately, not all the questions you have to face in practice can be answered so easily. Much more often, Business Intelligence has to operate on a larger dataset than one comprised by a single relational table, at times aggregating information from disparate data sources. This is where you are unlikely to get away with SQL alone—sophisticated Business Intelligence tools like those that the Oracle Business Intelligence suite includes are required.

However, you should have no illusions about the capabilities of Business Intelligence. It is important to realize that Business Intelligence is not a magic black box that can derive information from nowhere, answering probing analytical questions from sparse datasets. There will be a significant difference in the accuracy of the information extracted, depending on how dense the underlying dataset is.

Answering business questions from your data

As stated above, the quantity and quality of the information you can obtain directly depends on the quantity and quality of the data available at your disposal. Not surprisingly, the more information you can collect, the more probing analytical questions you can answer.

To start with, let's look at a simple example. Suppose you need to analyze the results of a survey you conducted online to get some vital feedback from your customers. It turned out, however, that only one-tenth of the overall number of your customers participated. Of course, the information you will extract from the results of this survey cannot be considered comprehensive, as the opinion of the majority remains unclear and, therefore, only a sparse dataset has been analyzed.

If you consult a dictionary, you should see that 'sparse' is a synonym to 'scanty'. What this means here is that a sparse dataset has gaps. Say, you have sales figures for today and don't have them for yesterday and so on. However, for analysis purposes, you often need a dense dataset — one that contains no gaps. So **densification** is the process of filling gaps in a dataset.

While in the above example, a factor that complicated performing a quality analysis was that there was not enough incoming information; you will most likely in practice experience another kind of problem — composing the 'right' dataset from the sea of data available at your disposal. In terms of Oracle Discoverer, such datasets are called **workbooks** and represent business areas — collections of related information. Each workbook contains worksheets displaying data from the perspectives you want to view that data in, to obtain answers to your business questions. So when creating a workbook, you should include all the data structures required for building the worksheets you want.

Diagrammatically, the scenario involving Oracle Discoverer workbooks, each of which can be used to answer a certain set of business questions might look like the following diagram:

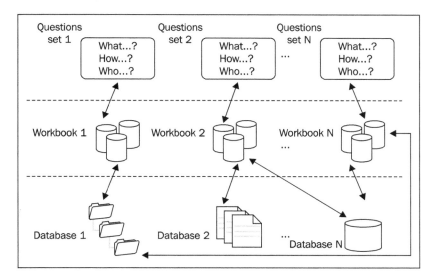

As you can see, Oracle Discoverer workbooks can be built on a variety of data sources, representing the derived data so that it can answer your business questions. The diagram in the figure gives you a rough idea of the mechanism used by Oracle Discoverer to provide a business view of the underlying data.

But you're probably wondering "How would I know which data structures must be included in a workbook to give enough information for getting those business questions answered?" Well, in most cases, the answer to this question is intuitively clear: you add to the workbook only those data structures that contain the data you want to see displayed at that point on the workbook's worksheets.

If you're working with relational data, then the rule of thumb is to include not only those tables whose data you want to see on worksheets, but also their related tables. It's not a big issue though, since the Discoverer wizard used to create a new workbook includes related tables by default. As you might guess, related tables may become required when the time comes to drill down through data to detail.

For example, when creating a workbook to be used for sales analysis, you would include at least the orders, customers, and employee tables. This is correct because you often need to have the ability to integrate customer, employee, and sales information for analysis. Now imagine that you want to create a worksheet for the report showing the sales of a particular region. What this means simply is that the regions table must also have been included.

 However, this may not be necessary if you're going to include only the region_id field in your report. Being part of the customers table, this field serves as the foreign key that relates to the regions table.

In terms of Oracle Discoverer, database tables included in a workbook are folders, each of which includes items representing columns of the corresponding table. It's interesting to note, however, that folders and items are not necessarily based on relational tables and their columns respectively — other data structure options, such as LDAP directories and entries are also possible. So, the Oracle Discoverer documentation defines a folder as a collection of closely related information, and an item can be thought of as a piece of information of a certain type, within a folder.

Comparing and analyzing data

Now that you have a rough idea of how data can be organized for business analysis, it's time to move on and look at how you might use that data to your advantage, gaining a comprehensive view of your business.

As we have just seen, within a workbook consolidating a collection of related information, you can create a set of worksheets, each of which is to answer a certain business question. Continuing the discussion, this section touches briefly on issues related to comparing and analyzing data.

To view the data displayed on a worksheet from the perspective you need, Oracle Discoverer offers a number of components, including totals, percentages, exceptions, and calculations. With these tools in hand, you'll be able to analyze data more quickly and easily.

Schematically, this might look like the following figure:

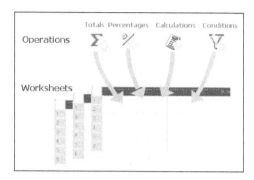

The above diagram illustrates that you can add totals, percentages, calculations, and filters to a worksheet through the corresponding Discoverer components. All these Discoverer tools are easy to use, and allow you to rearrange the worksheet's data or drill into it, so that you can see it from another perspective, with just a few clicks. In the *Asking business questions using data-access tools* section earlier in this chapter, you saw an example of how easy it is to calculate a total for a column on a worksheet.

Although Discoverer tools open up a great way to approach the problem of analyzing data, you may sometimes have to rearrange data even before it is included into a workbook. For example, in the area of comparative analyses, you may need to perform data densification before you can proceed to data analysis.

As usual, this can be best understood by example. Say, when performing a period-to-period comparison, you may face the problem of sparse data. For example, you perform day-to-day comparisons to see the inventory figures for various products on a daily basis. The problem is that the inventory table usually stores a row for a product when its quantity of available units changes. So, the rows stored in the inventory table might look like the following:

```
PROD_id EVENT_DT QUANT
------- --------- -----
111     05-FEB-10 15
111     08-FEB-10 7
222     05-FEB-10 17
222     07-FEB-10 14
333     05-FEB-10 7
333     08-FEB-10 25
```

As you can see, there are days when no event happened, and therefore, what you have here is a sparse dataset. In reports that you might want to create based on this table, you will most likely need this data to be represented differently, as a dense dataset. So, before you can include it to a workbook, a densification is needed.

The simplest way to solve this problem is to create a view based on the inventory table, so that the view contains a dense dataset. The densification might be accomplished with the help of the LAST_VALUE Oracle SQL analytic function, included in the select list of the view's SELECT statement.

The above example illustrated that the process of converting data into information you need, may start even before that data is chosen to be processed by a Business Intelligence tool. In other words, you may need to make some preparations to rearrange an underlying dataset so that it's ready for analysis.

 The downside to the above approach is the lack of flexibility. However, Oracle Discoverer gives you a greater degree of flexibility.

If you need the inventory table's original rows, you'll need to make a change to the set of underlying data objects. However, Oracle Discoverer provides a better option. Windowing functions, such as LAST_VALUE discussed here, can be used to compute aggregates with the help of calculations, a Discoverer analysis feature mentioned at the beginning of this section. Like other Discoverer analysis features, calculations can be activated or deactivated with a single click, thus giving you a greater degree of flexibility. The Oracle Discoverer features will be discussed in more detail later in this book.

Accessing transactional and dimensional data

It's interesting to note that a Business Intelligence system can work directly with transactional data, dealing with data reflecting current business operations. From the Business Intelligence's standpoint, though, not only current, but also the historical view of business operations is important.

Reporting against a transactional database

It's often the case that transactional data is stored in a relational database. Relational tables represent relational entities, such as products, orders, details, and customers, storing information about current transactions. As mentioned, a Business Intelligence solution can be built directly upon such a transactional system, containing data that you can use for analysis and reporting.

 You might be asking yourself: isn't dimensional data what Business Intelligence is all about? Well, like figure skating is not only about jumps, Business Intelligence is not only about multidimensional cubes. Rather, it's about answering analytical business questions, deriving information from both relational and dimensional sources.

It's important to understand, though, that a transactional system should remain mobile and highly responsive, enabling new transactions to be processed and stored quickly. So, a common problem with such systems is that they are not designed to store large amounts of data—old data should be removed from time to time.

While data set optimization is good for a transactional system as the performance increases, it's not so good for analysis and reporting purposes. This is why Business Intelligence solutions are often built upon a data warehouse, consolidating both old and new data that can actually be stored in different sources.

Using historical data

Like a transactional system, a data warehouse represents a relational database. Unlike a transactional system however, a warehouse accumulates data, which represents the business history of an organization, and is structured for reporting, analysis, and decision support. In warehouses, data is organized around business entities such as products, regions, and customers.

Data in a warehouse can be organized so that it concentrates on a certain subject matter, say, purchasing; that is, it's optimized to simplify the task of finding answers to questions about purchasing. So, aside from historical data, a warehouse often uses summaries containing pre-processed data to speed up access to frequently queried information.

Using historical data can provide a clearer picture of the status of your business, leading to improved predictive capabilities. As you might guess, historical data is derived from a transactional system that often cannot afford to keep large amounts of data due to performance requirements. In fact, Business Intelligence can utilize both transactional and historical data sources for reporting and analysis purposes.

Diagrammatically, this might look like the following diagram:

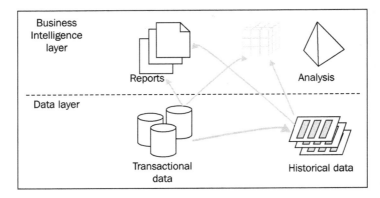

It's interesting to note that although transactional data is not stored in a warehouse, many Business Intelligence tools access that data through a warehouse, taking advantage of summaries and other warehouse features. Warehousing for analysis and reporting will be discussed in more detail in *Chapter 5, Warehousing for Analysis and Reporting*, later in this book.

Aggregating dimensional data

A multidimensional data model is often used to perform complex analysis of historical data. Multidimensional data is named so because it is organized by dimensions, such as products, times, customers, regions, and departments. Although there may be more than three dimensions in such data structures, they are often referred to as cubes.

The following diagram illustrates a cube that contains sales figures for groups of products for each month of Q4 in different regions.

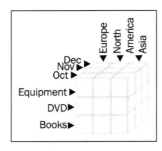

What you can see in the figure is a three-dimensional data structure, enabling you to concentrate on solving a particular business problem. Looking at this structure, you might wonder what operations can be applied to it. Operations often applied to multidimensional data to extract meaningful information include the following:

- Pivoting
- Drilling
- Sorting
- Filtering

These techniques will be discussed in detail in later chapters of this book.

Summary

The main purpose of this introductory chapter was to give you a taste of things to come. After reading the chapter, you should now have a clear understanding of what Business Intelligence is about. In particular, you should have learned that Business Intelligence allows you to better understand the meaning of the information you're gathering, answering the questions about the current status of your business, how it got to be where it is, and where it is headed.

You looked at some basic ideas underlying Business Intelligence, including those related to answering business questions from data, and accessing transactional and historical data. Through a simple example, you learned how easy it is to get an analytical question answered with Oracle BI Discoverer Plus, a powerful Business Intelligence tool from the Oracle Business Intelligence suite.

In the last sections of the chapter, you not only learned about what data Business Intelligence deals with, but also how this data is structured, and what are common techniques often applied to these data structures.

Throughout the next chapter, you'll learn all the necessary steps to install and configure the Oracle Business Intelligence components included within the Oracle Business Intelligence and Oracle Business Intelligence Tools suites.

2
Introducing Oracle Business Intelligence

You know by now that Oracle Business Intelligence allows you to go beyond simple database-driven applications with the help of SQL queries to derive information from the data being collected and stored. Oracle Business Intelligence is implemented as a collection of components grouped into suites, which are part of either Oracle Application Server or Oracle Fusion Middleware. As you will learn in this chapter, however, Oracle Business Intelligence is not limited to those components alone. Oracle Database also provides a number of natively supported Business Intelligence features, such as data warehousing, **Online Analytical Processing (OLAP)**, and analytic SQL functions. These features will be discussed in more detail in the next chapter, as well as in *Chapter 5, Warehousing for Analysis and Reporting*, which is dedicated to data warehousing.

This chapter covers getting up and running with Oracle Business Intelligence, including the following topics:

- Understanding Oracle Business Intelligence components
- Installing Oracle Business Intelligence suite
- Installing Oracle Business Intelligence Tools suite
- Configuring the Business Intelligence components
- Building a Business Intelligence system on top of Oracle Database
- Initial steps in exploring Oracle Business Intelligence

What Oracle Business Intelligence is comprised of

In the preceding chapter, you saw a brief example of the Oracle Discoverer Plus, an Oracle Business Intelligence component, in action. As mentioned previously, this chapter will discuss the components included in the Oracle Business Intelligence and Oracle Business Intelligence Tools suites in more detail, including their installation. Before proceeding to the installation though, let's take a closer look at the Oracle Business Intelligence components, trying to determine "what is what" within it.

Oracle Business Intelligence components

To start with, let's determine what kind of problems the Oracle Business Intelligence components are designed to solve. The following list enumerates these problems:

- Structuring data for analysis
- Analyzing data
- Creating reports
- Viewing and sharing reports

Now, you might wonder what Oracle Business Intelligence components are available and which problem each of them is designed to solve. The following is a list of the most popular components designed for analysis and reporting, which are included in the Oracle Business Intelligence package:

- *Oracle Discoverer Plus Relational* for analyzing relational data and creating reports
- *Oracle Discoverer Plus OLAP* for analyzing multidimensional data and creating reports
- *Oracle Discoverer Viewer* for reporting and publishing
- *Oracle Discoverer Portlet Provider* for publishing existing Discoverer reports to OracleAS Portal
- *Oracle Reports* for reporting and publishing

In addition, there are some useful tools in the Oracle Business Intelligence Tools package:

- *Oracle Discoverer Administrator* for structuring data for analysis
- *Oracle Warehouse Builder* for designing and deploying data warehouses, data marts, and Business Intelligence applications

- *Oracle Discoverer Desktop* for analyzing relational data and creating reports, which is a Windows-only application
- *Oracle Reports Developer* for building and publishing reports
- *Oracle Spreadsheet Add-In* for sharing data, making it possible for you to work with Oracle OLAP data in MS Excel

As you can see, some components included in the Oracle Business Intelligence Tools package are required to prepare data for analysis. While others, like those included in the Oracle Business Intelligence package, are designed for analysis, reporting, and sharing.

 The Oracle Business Intelligence and Oracle Business Intelligence Tools packages discussed here are part of Oracle Application Server 10*g* Release 2. Most of them, though, can also be found in the Portal, Forms, Reports, and Discoverer suite, which is part of Oracle Fusion Middleware 11*g*R1.

Before moving on, it would be interesting to note that Oracle Business Intelligence is not limited to the above packages only. For example, Oracle Database is not, strictly speaking, an Oracle Business Intelligence component, but still provides a number of important Business Intelligence features.

Although Oracle Business Intelligence can work with data derived from many different data sources, you'll be able to get the most out of it when it sits on top of an Oracle database, leveraging the Oracle database features and options related to dealing with business data. For example, you might build a powerful data warehouse environment based on Oracle Database, taking advantage of pre-built features such as the transportation, transformation, and loading (ETL) solution, OLAP engine, materialized views, and analytic SQL functions.

Composing a Business Intelligence system

Now that you know what components can be found in a Business Intelligence system, how might you build one? Actually, there may be more than one way to build a Business Intelligence system, using the Oracle Business Intelligence components discussed here. The fact is that there is some overlap in functionality between components when it comes to solving particular business tasks.

For example, you might use Oracle Reports for reporting or alternatively, you might use Oracle Discoverer Plus for the same purpose. It's important to note though, that in spite of similar functionality, the set of features each component provides can differ from one another. For example, Oracle Reports provides more output format options, in comparison to Discoverer Plus.

On the other hand, Discoverer Plus has a lot of powerful features for data analysis. What is interesting is that Discoverer Plus enables you to export worksheets to Oracle Reports so that you can enhance the worksheet data, taking advantage of the Oracle Reports' reporting features. So what we have here is a number of complementing features rather than simply an overlap in functionality.

Utilizing this concept of complementary components is precisely the method that should be employed when composing a Business Intelligence system—by grouping complementary Business Intelligence components together, you can implement a workflow that suits you best.

The following diagram illustrates a simple example of a Business Intelligence system built using Oracle Business Intelligence components:

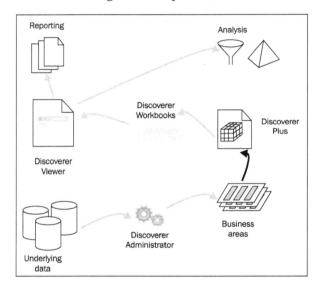

As you can see, the Business Intelligence system shown employs several Oracle Business components to convert data into information. It begins with **Discoverer Administrator,** which is used to create a business-oriented view of the underlying data, grouping that data into the so-called 'business areas'—collections of related information to be used by **Discoverer Plus** as input data. To make the data more suitable for analysis, Discoverer Plus allows you to organize it into worksheets, grouped in turn into workbooks.

You can also see **Discoverer Viewer** in the diagram. Although using this component is optional as long as Discoverer Plus is presented, it provides a more intuitive way of reporting and analysis. You have to be familiar only with a web browser to be able to quickly get started with analyzing data and preparing reports using the Discoverer Viewer tool.

Often, though, choosing one component over another may not only be a matter of taste. For example, Discoverer Administrator will be of no help if you have to work with multidimensional data rather than relational data. Moreover, Discoverer Administrator is a Windows-only tool. What this means simply is that you won't be able to use it on a non-Windows machine.

Suppose you want to analyze the data stored in a multidimensional data source, with Discoverer Plus OLAP. So, first make sure you have the data organized so that Discoverer Plus OLAP can use it. To achieve this, you might use Oracle Business Intelligence Warehouse Builder, allowing you to implement a data warehouse environment.

Warehouse Builder can read all kinds of data: operational data, historical data, and external data, which can be derived from disparate sources, including Oracle Database, ODBC, flat files, as well as many other non-Oracle database systems, such as SQL Server, Sybase, DB2, and Informix.

Once you have created a data warehouse, you can use it as input to Discoverer Plus OLAP, which in turn will generate Discoverer worksheets based on that input. Of course, you can be content with the analysis and reporting features of Discoverer Plus and go no further. Eventually, though, you might want to use the worksheets you created in Discoverer Plus in another Business Intelligence tool, such as Oracle Reports or Discoverer Viewer.

Diagrammatically, this might look like this:

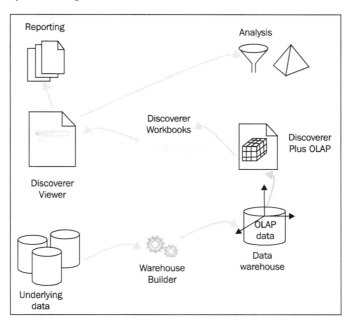

Looking at the diagram, you might wonder what underlying data can actually be. As mentioned earlier, Warehouse Builder can consolidate data from different sources—not necessarily just from an Oracle database. So, among other sources, Warehouse Builder can define appropriate OLAP metadata based on the data stored in many relational databases, Microsoft Excel spreadsheets, and even flat files.

Sitting on top of Oracle Database

As mentioned, Oracle Database offers a broad set of Business Intelligence features, which makes it ideal for a database backing a Business Intelligence solution. For example, you might build a data warehouse environment within an Oracle database, effectively extracting data from an operational environment and bringing it into an analytical one.

The following diagram gives a conceptual depiction of what a Business Intelligence system backed by an Oracle database might look like:

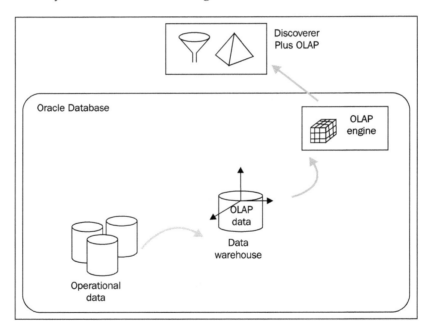

It's interesting to note that operational data can be derived not only from an Oracle database, but also from external sources. Data warehousing will be discussed in more detail later in this book.

Installing Oracle Business Intelligence software

The following sections will walk you through the steps necessary to obtain and install Oracle Business Intelligence software, which you will need in order to follow the examples throughout the rest of this book.

The software you will need

As mentioned, you have more than one option when it comes to Oracle Business Intelligence software. Currently, the two most popular options are the following:

- *Oracle Business Intelligence suite*, part of Oracle Application Server 10*g* Release 2
- *Portal, Forms, Reports, and Discoverer suite*, part of Oracle Fusion Middleware 11*g* Release 1

The first option—the Oracle Business Intelligence suite, part of Oracle Application Server 10*g* Release 2—includes the following components:

- Oracle Business Intelligence Discoverer
- Oracle HTTP Server
- Oracle Application Server Containers for J2EE (OC4J)
- Oracle Enterprise Manager 10*g* Application Server Control
- Oracle Application Server Web Cache
- Oracle Application Server Reports Services

The first component in the list above actually represents a group of components whose names start with Discoverer, including Discoverer Plus, Discoverer Portlet Provider, and Discoverer Viewer.

It's interesting to note that Discoverer Administrator is not included in the Oracle Business Intelligence suite package—it is part of the Oracle Business Intelligence Tools package. Another Discoverer component not included in the Oracle Business Intelligence package, but in the Oracle Business Intelligence Tools package, is Discoverer Desktop.

Another interesting software component presented in the previous list, which you might use for reporting on business data, is Reports Services.

You might wonder what the other components that are not directly related to Business Intelligence are doing in the Oracle Business Intelligence suite package. The answer is that they are required to satisfy dependencies of the Business Intelligence components included. If you recall, Oracle Business Intelligence suite is part of Oracle Application Server. What this means in practice is that the Business Intelligence applications included in the package, such as Discoverer, are Oracle Application Server applications, which, therefore, need an Oracle Application Server up and running to be deployed to. On the plus side, you don't need to install additional packages—everything you need is included.

Another option to take advantage of the same Business Intelligence tools (for example, Discoverer, Reports Services) is to install the Portal, Forms, Reports, and Discoverer suite, which is part of Oracle Fusion Middleware Fusion.

This package includes the following components:

- HTTP Server
- WebCache
- Portal
- Forms Services
- Forms Builder
- Reports Services
- Report Builder/Compiler
- Discoverer Administrator
- Discoverer Plus
- Discoverer Viewer
- Discoverer Services
- Discoverer Desktop
- Enterprise Manager Fusion Middleware Control

As you can see, the Portal, Forms, Reports, and Discoverer suite, like Oracle Business Intelligence suite, includes some components that are not directly related to Business Intelligence, but are required to satisfy dependencies of the Business Intelligence components included.

You might also notice that the Portal, Forms, Reports, and Discoverer suite, unlike Oracle Business Intelligence suite, includes Discoverer Administrator and Discoverer Desktop. So you won't need to install another package to obtain these components.

A major downside to choosing the Portal, Forms, Reports, and Discoverer suite, though, is that it requires some additional software to be installed in your system. Here is the list of the required additional software components:

- WebLogic Server
- Repository Creation Utility
- Identity Management
- SSO Metadata Repository Creation Assistant
- Patch Scripts
- Identity Management 10*g*R3
- Oracle Database

It is largely for this reason (in order to save you the trouble of installing a lot of software to be able to follow the examples in this book), that the *Installation process* section later in this chapter will cover the installation of Oracle Business Intelligence suite, part of Oracle Application Server 10*g* Release 2 rather than the Portal, Forms, Reports, and Discoverer suite of Oracle Fusion Middleware 11*g* Release 1.

Where to get the software

You can download the software discussed here from OTN's Software Downloads page at: `http://www.oracle.com/technology/software/index.html`. It's important to remember that each software component available from this page comes with a Development License, which allows for free download and unlimited evaluation time. This license is available at: `http://www.oracle.com/technology/software/popup-license/standard-license.html`.

Turning back to OTN's Software Downloads page, go to the Middleware section and, assuming you want to download Oracle Business Intelligence suite, click the **Business Intelligence SE** link to proceed to the Oracle Application Server 10*g* Release 2 (10.1.2.0.2) page at: `http://www.oracle.com/technology/software/products/ias/htdocs/101202.html`.

On this page, go down to the Business Intelligence section and find the links to the packages provided for your operating system. Each package is designed to be copied on a separate CD. The number of CDs, and the size of packages to be copied on them, may vary depending on the operating system. What you need to do is download the packages and then copy each to a CD.

Looking through the links, you may notice that Tools CD — the link to the package containing the Oracle Business Intelligence Tools suite — is available only for Microsoft Windows operating system. This is because the components included in the Oracle Business Intelligence Tools suite are **Windows-only applications**.

If, in place of the Oracle Business Intelligence suite, you want to download the Portal, Forms, Reports, and Discoverer suite, you have to follow the Oracle Fusion Middleware 11*g* R1 link that can be found in the Middleware section on OTN's Software Downloads page.

As a result, you'll move on to the Oracle Fusion Middleware 11*g*R1 Software Downloads page at: `http://www.oracle.com/technology/software/products/middleware/htdocs/fmw_11_download.html`.

On this page, move on to the Portal, Forms, Reports and Discoverer section and pick up the distribution divided into several packages. Again, the number of packages within a distribution, and their size, may vary depending on the operating system.

Installation process

This section provides a quick guide to installing the Oracle Business Intelligence suite, part of Oracle Application Server 10*g* Release 2.

To obtain a comprehensive installation guide for your operating system, you can refer to the Oracle documentation. You might start out by visiting OTN's Oracle Documentation page, available at: `http://www.oracle.com/technology/documentation/index.html`. Start with checking out prerequisites to avoid possible installation issues.

Here are the steps you need to perform in order to install the Oracle Business Intelligence suite on Windows (on other operating system platforms, the installation process is similar to this one):

1. Insert the CD labeled CD1 (assuming you marked the disks as they were marked on the download page) into your disk drive.
2. In the root directory of the CD, find and execute the `setup.exe` file. It starts the **Oracle Universal Installer**, checking first if the Installer requirements are met.

3. The first screen of the Oracle Universal Installer you should see is the **Welcome** screen, which should look like the following screenshot.

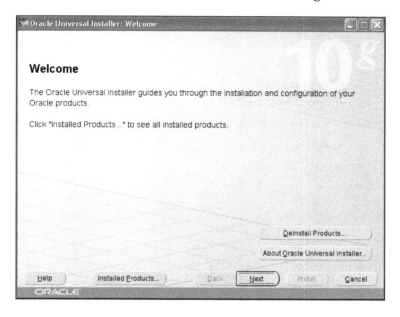

4. If you don't want to de-install Oracle products that might already be installed on your machine, click the **Next** button on the Welcome screen to move on to the next screen of the Installer, which is called **Specify File Locations**.

5. On the **Specify File Locations** screen, you can change the source to install the software from and/or the destination where you want to install it. You are unlikely to want to change the path to the source, because it's detected automatically. However, you will most likely want to change the destination folder.

6. Once you have set the paths on the **Specify File Locations** screen as needed, click **Next** to make the Installer analyze dependencies and continue with the installation.

 If the Installer detects an ORACLE_HOME environment variable set in your system, it will ask you to remove it and then re-start the installation again.

7. After analyzing dependencies, the Installer should open the **Language Selection** screen, where you can select the languages in which the product will run:

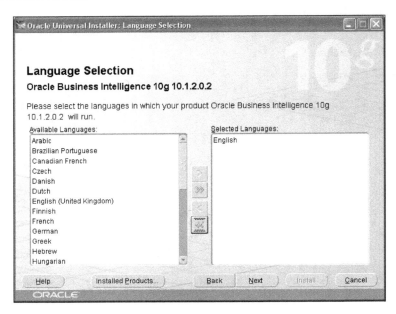

8. After you have selected the language or languages to be used, click **Next** to continue with the installation.

9. The next screen you should see is **Specify Port Configuration Options**, where you can specify whether you want to configure the Oracle Application Server ports manually or automatically. The default option is **Automatic**.

10. The next screen is **Provide Outgoing Mail Server Information**. If you're not planning to distribute reports via e-mail, you can leave it blank and click **Next**.

11. On the next screen called **Specify Instance Name** and **ias_admin Password**, you must specify the name for the Oracle Business Intelligence instance being installed, as well as the password for it:

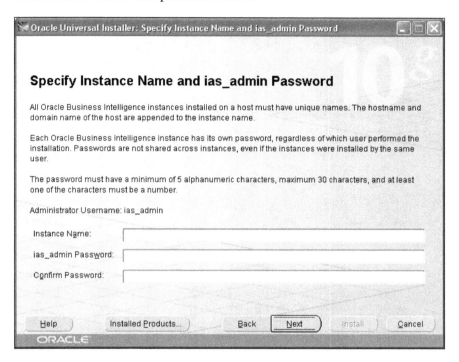

12. Once you have completed these fields, click **Next** to proceed.

13. The next screen is **Summary**, which summarizes the information about the current installation. In particular, it shows the languages you've chosen for the products being installed, global settings, space requirements, and finally the list of the products to be installed:

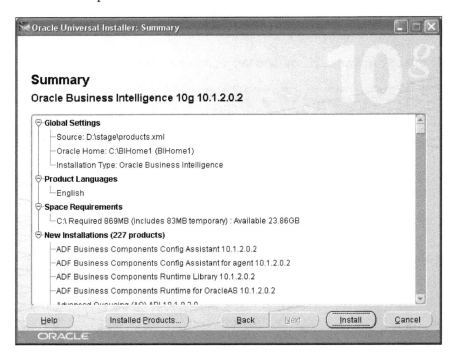

14. Having looked through the information in the **Summary** screen; you can go back to change the settings set at the preceding steps, by clicking the **Back** button. Otherwise, you can launch the installation process by clicking **Install**.

15. After you click **Install**, the Installer will open the **Install** screen that will provide you with the details of the installation for an Oracle Business Intelligence instance on your machine:

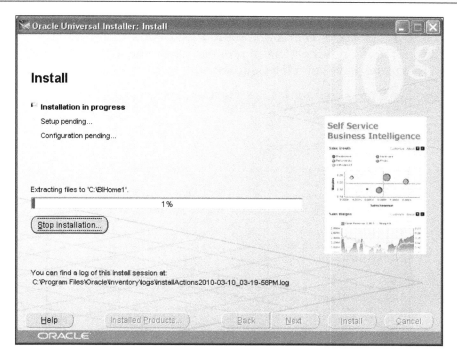

16. As you should see in the **Install** screen, the installation process consists of the following three phases:
    - ° Copying files
    - ° Setting up
    - ° Configuration

17. At some point, during the copying files stage, you'll be prompted to insert Oracle BI CD2 into your disk drive.

18. After the copying files stage has been completed successfully, the Installer will proceed to the setting up stage and ask you to insert Oracle BI CD1 again.

19. Once the setup process is completed, the Installer proceeds to the configuration stage. The **Configuration Assistants** screen appears, where you can see the configuring work in progress. It's highly recommended that all the assistants have completed successfully before you go any further:

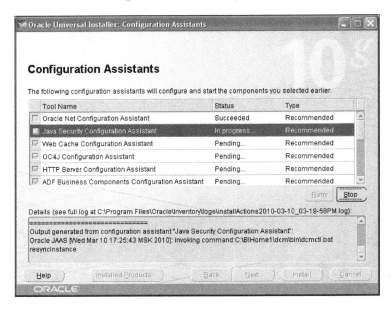

20. After all the assistants have completed successfully, you can click the **Next** button in the Configuration Assistants screen. As a result, the **End of Installation** screen shown should appear:

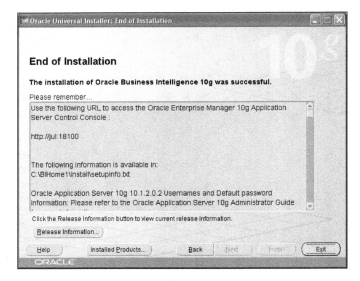

21. On the **End of Installation** screen, look through the information provided in the **Please remember ...** box, and click **Exit** to complete the installation and exit the Installer.

 You can always to look through this information later by viewing the bi_install_info.txt file, which you can find in the root directory of the installed product.

22. After you exit the Installer, the page entitled **Welcome to Oracle Business Intelligence** should be opened in your browser.

By now, you should have the Oracle Business Intelligence suite installed on your computer. This is not it, though. You may still need to install some additional software and perform post-installation tasks.

Installing the Oracle Business Intelligence Tools package

If you are a Windows user, it's highly recommended that you also install the Oracle Business Intelligence Tools package. As mentioned earlier in the chapter, the Tools installation package can be found in the Business Intelligence section at the Oracle Application Server download page—just another package to download in this section, labeled as "Tools CD". On this download page, in the Business Intelligence sections other than for Windows, this package is not available.

The following are the steps for installing the Oracle Business Intelligence Tools suite on your machine:

1. Insert the CD labeled Tools CD into your disk drive.

2. The root directory of the Tools CD contains the autorun.inf file, which means the setup.exe should be launched automatically. If **AutoRun** is disabled in your system, launch setup.exe manually.

3. As with an Oracle Business Intelligence suite installation, this installation is managed by the Oracle Universal Installer. If the Installer requirements are met, the first screen you should see is the **Welcome** screen—the same one you saw earlier in this chapter. To move on to the next screen, just click the **Next** button.

4. The next screen is the **Specify File Locations** screen, where you can change the paths to the source and destination of the installation. Then, click **Next** to continue.

5. On the next screen called **Select Installation Type,** you have to select the type of installation you want. The options are the following:

   ○ Business User

   ○ Administrator/Power User

   ○ Developer

   ○ Custom

> Probably the best way to make sure you'll get all you need from the installation is to choose the **Custom** option, which allows you to manually choose which components to install.

6. On the **Select Installation Type** screen, also make sure to select the product languages in the **Language Selection dialog,** which you can launch by clicking on the **Product Languages** button.

7. On the **Available Product Components** screen that appears in the case of choosing **Custom** on the preceding screen, select components you want to include to your installation, and then click **Next** to proceed.

   At this stage, you can easily exclude the components that you won't need. For example, if you don't use JDeveloper, you won't need the Oracle Business Intelligence Beans (for JDeveloper) component.

8. The next screen you should see is **Provide Outgoing Mail Server Information,** which you can leave blank if you're not going to distribute reports via e-mail.

9. At this point, you should reach the **Summary** screen, detailing all the information about the current installation. You have two options here: **Install** and **Back**. Choose the former to launch the installation of an Oracle Business Intelligence Tools instance on your machine, or the latter to go back and change the parameters of the installation.

10. After **Install** is clicked on the **Summary** screen, the Installer opens the **Install** screen to keep you informed about the installation process details. As with the Oracle Business Intelligence suite installation, this installation consists of the following three phases:

    ○ Copying files

    ○ Setting up

    ○ Configuration

11. At the configuration stage, the **Configuration Assistants** screen should appear. The only configuration assistant to go through should be the Oracle Net Configuration Assistant, whose wizard should be automatically launched. The first screen of the Oracle Net Configuration Assistant is a **Welcome** screen.

12. On the **Welcome** screen of the **Net Configuration Assistant** wizard, click **Next**. As a result, you should immediately move on to the **Done** screen, the last screen of the wizard.

13. On the **Done** screen of the Net Configuration Assistant, click **Finish**, which should close the Net Configuration Assistant wizard.

14. After the Net Configuration Assistant wizard is complete, the **End of Installation** screen of the Installer should appear. In this screen, click **Exit** to complete the installation.

15. After you exit the Installer, the page entitled **Welcome to Oracle Business Intelligence Tools** should be automatically opened in your browser.

This completes the installation of a Business Intelligence Tools instance on your computer. Before you can use it, however, some post-installation tasks need to be completed.

Post-installation tasks

Once you have downloaded and installed the Oracle Business Intelligence and Oracle Business Intelligence Tools packages, make sure that you have the database engine they need up and running.

> Of course, the list of post-installation tasks to perform may vary depending on the tasks you're planning to solve with the Business Intelligence solution just installed. Whatever tasks you're planning, though, your Business Intelligence solution most likely will sit on top of a database. So, your first step, as mentioned previously, is to make sure that there is a database server in your system working properly. The examples throughout this book assume that you have an Oracle database 10g or later installed on your system.

Looking at the post-installation tasks from a practical point of view, let's try to figure out what you need to do in order to quickly get started with the software components just installed.

Suppose you want to do some work in Discoverer Plus, analyzing relational data stored in the underlying database. Before you can do that, though, you must have access to an **EUL (End User Layer)**, which contains metadata to access the database data, and is intended to isolate you from database complexity. One way to define an EUL is through the Discoverer Administrator tool, which is part of the Oracle Business Intelligence Tools suite.

If you're not a Windows user, Discoverer Administrator is not among your options—as well as all the other tools from the Oracle Business Intelligence Tools package. In this case, you might create an EUL with the Discoverer EUL Command Line for Java instead. This tool is part of the Oracle Business Intelligence suite.

To be able to connect to Discoverer Administrator, make sure you have a net service name for the underlying database defined in the tnsnames.ora file, which should be located in the BITools_Home/network/admin directory.

While this task can be performed manually by editing the tnsnames.ora file with a text editor, the following steps describe how you might solve it with the Net Configuration Assistant visual tool instead:

1. Launch **Net Configuration Assistant** by clicking **Start | Programs | Oracle-BIToolsHome1 | Configuration and Migration Tools | Net Configuration Assistant**.

Be careful with what tnsnames.ora file you're editing. Note that clicking the previous path link will invoke **Net Configuration Assistant** associated with the tnsnames.ora file located in the BI_Home/network/admin directory, which is not what you need here.

This should start the **Net Configuration Assistant** wizard, opening its first screen as shown next:

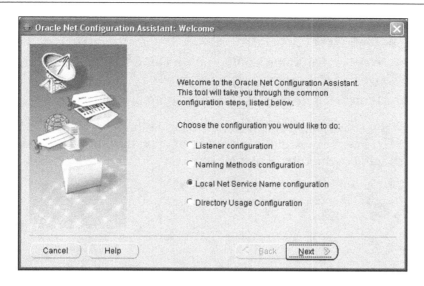

2. On the **Welcome** screen of the assistant, choose **Local Net Service Name configuration**, and click **Next**.

3. The next screen you should see is called **Net Service Name Configuration**, in which you should select **Add**, and click **Next**.

4. On the **Net Service Name Configuration**, the **Service Name** screen appears next, where you'll be prompted to enter the service name of your Oracle database. If you have, for example Oracle Database XE, this could be XE.

5. On the next screen, called **Net Service Name Configuration, Select Protocols**, choose a protocol to communicate with the database across the network and click **Next**.

6. On the **Net Service Name Configuration, TCP/IP Protocol** screen, specify the host name of the computer where the database is installed, as well as the port number, and click **Next**.

7. On the **Net Service Name Configuration, Test** screen, you can select **Yes, perform a test** to test that a connection can be made, or **No, do not test** and click **Next** to skip to the next screen.

8. On the **Net Service Name Configuration, Net Service Name** screen, provide the Net Service Name, say, XE, and then click **Next**.

9. On the **Net Service Name Configuration, Another Net Service** screen, select **No** and click **Next**.

10. On the **Net Service Name Configuration Done** screen, click **Next**. This will bring back the **Welcome** screen of the wizard.

11. On the **Welcome** screen, click **Finish** to complete the configuration steps.

As a result of the above steps, the tnsnames.ora file should appear in the BITools_Home/network/admin directory. If you open this file with a text editor, you should see the entry looking like this:

```
# tnsnames.ora Network Configuration File: C:\oracle\BIToolsHome_1\
network\admin\tnsnames.ora
# Generated by Oracle configuration tools.

XE =
  (DESCRIPTION =
    (ADDRESS_LIST =
      (ADDRESS = (PROTOCOL = TCP)(HOST = yul)(PORT = 1521))
    )
    (CONNECT_DATA =
      (SERVICE_NAME = XE)
    )
  )
```

Now that you have defined a net service name for the underlying database in the BITool's tnsnames.ora file, you can move on and create an EUL with Discoverer Administrator. Here are the steps:

1. Launch **Discoverer Administrator** by clicking **Start | Programs | Oracle Business Intelligence Tools-BIToolsHome1 | Oracle Discoverer Administrator**.

2. In the modal dialog **Connect to Oracle Business Intelligence Discoverer Administrator**, you'll be prompted to enter a username/password pair to connect to the database, as well as the database service name you specified when creating net service name configuration, as described in the preceding steps.

3. Once you have specified the information required to connect to the database and clicked **Connect**, Discoverer Administrator will ask you to create an EUL, because you do not have access to one. Click **Yes** to create one.

4. As a result, the **EUL Manager** dialog should appear:

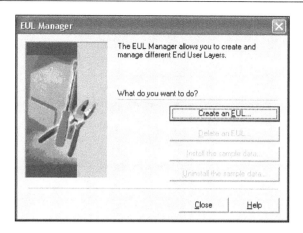

5. In the **EUL Manager** dialog, click the **Create an EUL ...** button to proceed to creating a new EUL. This will launch the **Create EUL** Wizard.

6. On the first step of the **Create EUL** Wizard, you can select a user from the list of database users. This can be done in the **Select User** dialog, which you can open by clicking the **Select ...** button on the wizard screen.

7. In the **Select User** dialog, click **Go** to see a list of all the users available. Choose one by double-clicking it. For example, you might choose the HR user as it represents a demonstration schema installed with an Oracle database by default.

8. After a user has been selected, the **Finish** button in the **Create EUL Wizard** should become available. Click it to make Discoverer Administrator create the EUL. This process will go on behind the scenes and should take less than a minute. Once it's completed, you should see a message informing you about it.

9. Close the **EUL Manager** dialog by clicking **Close**.

You just created an EUL, but that's not it. Before you can connect to Discoverer Plus, you may need to create an entry for the underlying database in the tnsnames.ora file, located in the BI_Home/network/admin directory. The steps are similar to those you performed to define a net service name for this same database in the BITool's tnsnames.ora file, as discussed earlier in this section.

The only difference is that you have to launch the BIHome's Net Configuration Assistant rather than BIToolsHome's one. So you should launch it by clicking **Start | Programs | Oracle-BIHome1 | Configuration and Migration Tools | Net Configuration Assistant**.

Finally, you can connect to Discoverer Plus. To launch Discoverer, point your browser to the following URL: `http://yourhostname:7777/discoverer/plus`. This should output the login page:

The **User Name** and **Password** fields in the above login form assume you provide a database username and its password, respectively. For example, you might use the `hr/hr` pair to connect to a standard demonstration schema installed by default with an Oracle Database installation. In the **Database** field, you have to specify the service name for the database, as defined in the `tnsnames.ora` file. And in the **End User Layer** field, you can specify the name of the EUL you created earlier. For more detail, you can refer to the Connect to OracleBI Discoverer page help topic, which you can invoke by clicking the help link on the login page.

Summary

In this chapter, you learned how to install and configure an Oracle Business Intelligence solution. In particular, you walked through the steps of installing the Oracle Business Intelligence suite and Oracle Business Intelligence Tools suite, including configuration steps discussed in the "Post-installation tasks" section.

You should now have Oracle Business Intelligence components installed and ready to work on your computer. In the next chapter, we'll step aside and take a look at the Oracle Database Business Intelligence features. Then, in Chapter 4, we'll come back to the Business Intelligence components discussed in this chapter.

3
Working with Database Data

As mentioned earlier, Oracle Business Intelligence is not limited to only the Oracle Application Server solutions discussed in the preceding chapter. Oracle Database itself has a lot to offer when it comes to Business Intelligence. To better understand which Oracle Database features can be regarded as Business Intelligence features, it would be wise to recall what Business Intelligence is all about. Returning to the discussion about the Business Intelligence basics in *Chapter 1*, you might recall that Business Intelligence is first of all about answering analytical business questions.

So, if you've got used to visual tools, this chapter encourages you to branch out of your comfort zone, and gives you a chance to understand manually written SQL code. You might be surprised as to just how much SQL can offer when it comes to answering analytical business questions based on the data you have stored in the database, as well as in external sources.

In this chapter, you will learn to do the following:

- Use analytic SQL functions to answer business questions
- Perform multidimensional data analysis through the prism of SQL
- Leverage the computational power of Oracle Database
- Understand database structures behind Business Intelligence metadata components

Using analytic SQL functions

Analytic SQL is one of those Oracle Database native features that you can start using immediately after installing the database. Of course, you will also need some data stored in the database to play with. However, the data available in the demonstration database schemas can be quite enough to begin with.

Answering simple questions

As stated earlier, there are business questions that can be answered with a simple SQL query issued against the database. Questions starting with "how many" are a good example. Often, to answer such questions, you can use the COUNT SQL function. For example, you might need to know how many employees in your organization have been working for the company for 15 years or more. In this example, you might query the employees table located in the hr/hr demonstration schema, issuing the following statement:

```
SELECT count(*) FROM employees WHERE (EXTRACT(YEAR FROM (SYSDATE)) -
EXTRACT(YEAR FROM (hire_date))) >= 15;
```

The output should look like this:

```
  COUNT(*)
----------
        17
```

The previous code tells you that there are 17 records satisfying the criterion.

Multidimensional data analysis with SQL

It's important to realize that SQL can be used to answer not only simple questions like the one discussed in the preceding section. Using advanced SQL features, you can even perform multidimensional data analysis as well, enabling you to answer complex analytical questions.

This can be best understood by an example on group operations, aggregating data over multiple rows stored in several tables. Suppose you collect information about sales, storing the data in related tables within a single database schema. At the end of each quarter, you need to know the summarized sales figures for every region, for each month within that quarter.

To start with, let's create a new database schema, and the tables within it that are needed for this example. You can perform all these tasks from SQL*Plus. First, you have to launch SQLPLUS. This can be done from within an operating system prompt as follows:

```
C:\oracle\...>sqlplus
```

When prompted, you have to connect as sysdba:

```
Enter user-name: /as sysdba
```

From now on, the key SQL code presented in this chapter can also be found in the downloadable archive accompanying this book. You can find it at the book's page on the Packt website.

Once connected as sysdba, you can issue the following statements to create a new schema and grant it the privileges required for this example:

```
CREATE USER usr IDENTIFIED BY usr;

GRANT connect, resource TO usr;

CONN usr/usr
```

Before you can proceed to the example, you need to define some tables in the newly created database schema. For example, you might create the following tables: salespersons, regions, and orders related to one another through the foreign keys defined in the orders table. Here is the SQL code to issue:

```
CREATE TABLE salespersons (
  emp_id    VARCHAR2(10) PRIMARY KEY,
  emp_name    VARCHAR2(40)
);

CREATE TABLE regions (
  reg_id    VARCHAR2(2) PRIMARY KEY,
  reg_name    VARCHAR2(20)
);

CREATE TABLE orders(
  ordno    NUMBER PRIMARY KEY,
  empid    VARCHAR2(10) REFERENCES salespersons(emp_id),
  regid    VARCHAR2(2) REFERENCES regions(reg_id),
  orddate DATE,
  total    NUMBER(10,2)
);
```

Next, you have to populate these tables with some data, so that you can perform queries against them. As the `orders` table refers to the `salespersons` and `regions` tables, you first have to populate these two tables with data. You might use the following statements for this:

```
INSERT INTO salespersons VALUES ('violet', 'Violet Robinson');

INSERT INTO salespersons VALUES ('maya', 'Maya Silver');

INSERT INTO regions VALUES ('NA', 'North America');

INSERT INTO regions VALUES ('EU', 'Europe');
```

Now that you have filled up the `salespersons` and `regions` tables, you can move on and populate the `orders` table:

 The following code assumes that your session uses the `DD-MON-YY` date format by default. If it's not the case, you may get an error such as `ORA-01843` or `ORA-01858`. To see your session default date format, you can issue the following query: `SELECT * FROM nls_session_ parameters WHERE PARAMETER = 'NLS_DATE_FORMAT';` and then correct the following queries accordingly.

```
INSERT INTO orders VALUES
(1001, 'violet', 'NA', '10-JAN-2010', 1450.00);

INSERT INTO orders VALUES
(1002, 'violet', 'NA', '15-JAN-2010', 2310.00);

INSERT INTO orders VALUES
(1003, 'maya', 'EU', '20-JAN-2010', 1480.00);

INSERT INTO orders VALUES
(1004, 'violet', 'NA', '19-FEB-2010', 3700.00);

INSERT INTO orders VALUES
(1005, 'maya', 'EU', '24-FEB-2010', 1850.00);

INSERT INTO orders VALUES
(1006, 'maya', 'EU', '04-MAR-2010', 1770.00);

INSERT INTO orders VALUES
(1007, 'maya', 'EU', '05-MAR-2010', 1210.50);
```

```
INSERT INTO orders VALUES
(1008, 'violet', 'NA', '05-MAR-2010', 10420.00);

COMMIT;
```

You now have all the parts required to proceed with the example, and can issue a query that summarizes sales figures for every region for each month. Here is what this query might look like:

```
SELECT r.reg_name region, TO_CHAR(TO_DATE(EXTRACT(MONTH FROM (o.orddat
e)),'MM'),'Month') month, SUM(o.total) sales
FROM regions r, orders o
WHERE r.reg_id = o.regid
GROUP BY ROLLUP(EXTRACT(MONTH FROM (o.orddate)), r.reg_name);
```

In the above query, you summarize the data representing the sales figures, generating subtotals for every region for each month, and then totals for each month with the help of the GROUP BY ... ROLLUP clause. The query results should look like this:

```
REGION                 MONTH         SALES
-------------------- --------- ----------
Europe                 January        1480
North America          January        3760
                       January        5240
Europe                 February       1850
North America          February       3700
                       February       5550
Europe                 March        2980.5
North America          March         10420
                       March       13400.5
                                    24190.5
```

As you can see, the query output contains not only monthly sales per region and month totals for each month, but also the grand total, which is nothing but the sum of the month totals. You might exclude this grand total from the report if you are using a partial ROLLUP as shown next:

```
SELECT r.reg_name region, TO_CHAR(TO_DATE(EXTRACT(MONTH FROM (o.orddat
e)),'MM'),'Month') month, SUM(o.total) sales
FROM regions r, orders o
WHERE r.reg_id = o.regid
GROUP BY EXTRACT(MONTH FROM (o.orddate)), ROLLUP(r.reg_name);
```

As the month field is excluded from the ROLLUP here, the month totals will not be summarized:

```
REGION               MONTH       SALES
-------------------  ---------  ----------
Europe               January       1480
North America        January       3760
                     January       5240
Europe               February      1850
North America        February      3700
                     February      5550
Europe               March       2980.5
North America        March        10420
                     March      13400.5
```

Changing the order in which the parameters of ROLLUP appear will also affect the report. In our example, if you move the r.reg_name parameter to the first position, the report will generate totals for each region rather than for each month. Here is the query:

```
SELECT r.reg_name region, TO_CHAR(TO_DATE(EXTRACT(MONTH FROM (o.orddat
e)),'MM'),'Month') month, SUM(o.total) sales
FROM regions r, orders o
WHERE r.reg_id = o.regid
GROUP BY ROLLUP(r.reg_name, EXTRACT(MONTH FROM (o.orddate)));
```

Here is its output:

```
REGION               MONTH       SALES
-------------------  ---------  ----------
Europe               January       1480
Europe               February      1850
Europe               March       2980.5
Europe                            6310.5
North America        January       3760
North America        February     ·3700
North America        March        10420
North America                     17880
                                 24190.5
```

As you can see, in the above report there are no longer any month totals. Instead, it provides you with the totals for each region.

Cubing

In the preceding section, you looked at several examples of how you can summarize sales figures, playing with totals and subtotals. In particular, you saw how the ROLLUP function can be used to produce the totals for either each month or each region, as well as the overall total in either case.

So by now you are probably wondering if it's possible to have the totals for both each month and each region, thus having all possible combinations of the grouping columns within a single report. While there is more than one way to achieve this, using the CUBE extension of the GROUP BY clause is the most elegant and effective one.

The following figure gives a graphical depiction of how CUBE differs from ROLLUP when it comes to generating summary information:

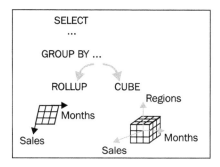

Switching to SQL, you might write the following query using the CUBE function in the GROUP BY clause:

```
SELECT r.reg_name region, TO_CHAR(TO_DATE(EXTRACT(MONTH FROM (o.orddat
e)),'MM'),'Month') month, SUM(o.total) sales
FROM regions r, orders o
WHERE r.reg_id = o.regid
GROUP BY CUBE(EXTRACT(MONTH FROM (o.orddate)), r.reg_name);
```

The previous query should generate the following report:

REGION	MONTH	SALES
Europe	January	1480
North America	January	3760
	January	5240
Europe	February	1850
North America	February	3700
	February	5550
Europe	March	2980.5
North America	March	10420
	March	13400.5
Europe		6310.5
North America		17880
		24190.5

As you can see, you now have all possible subtotals and totals combinations presented in the report. This is why changing the order of columns in CUBE won't affect the report, unlike with ROLLUP. So, the following query should actually give you the same results as above:

```
SELECT r.reg_name region, TO_CHAR(TO_DATE(EXTRACT(MONTH FROM (o.orddat
e)),'MM'),'Month') month, SUM(o.total) sales
FROM regions r, orders o
WHERE r.reg_id = o.regid
GROUP BY CUBE(r.reg_name, EXTRACT(MONTH FROM (o.orddate)));
```

However, the order of rows in the report will be a little different:

```
REGION               MONTH       SALES
-------------------- --------- ----------
Europe               January        1480
Europe               February       1850
Europe               March        2980.5
Europe                            6310.5
North America        January        3760
North America        February       3700
North America        March         10420
North America                     17880
                     January        5240
                     February       5550
                     March       13400.5
                                 24190.5
```

Just as there is a partial ROLLUP, there is also a partial CUBE. For example, you might issue the following query:

```
SELECT r.reg_name region, TO_CHAR(TO_DATE(EXTRACT(MONTH FROM (o.orddat
e)),'MM'),'Month') month, SUM(o.total) sales
FROM regions r, orders o
WHERE r.reg_id = o.regid
GROUP BY r.reg_name, CUBE(EXTRACT(MONTH FROM (o.orddate)));
```

This should generate the following output:

```
REGION               MONTH       SALES
-------------------- --------- ----------
Europe               January        1480
Europe               February       1850
Europe               March        2980.5
Europe                            6310.5
North America        January        3760
North America        February       3700
North America        March         10420
North America                     17880
```

As you can see, it only includes the totals for each region, and not for each month. Interestingly, you would get the same results if you replaced CUBE with ROLLUP, issuing the following query:

```
SELECT r.reg_name region, TO_CHAR(TO_DATE(EXTRACT(MONTH FROM (o.orddat
e)),'MM'),'Month') month, SUM(o.total) sales
FROM regions r, orders o
WHERE r.reg_id = o.regid
GROUP BY r.reg_name, ROLLUP(EXTRACT(MONTH FROM (o.orddate)));
```

Thus, a one column CUBE operation produces the same results as the identical ROLLUP operation.

Generating reports with only summary rows

In some cases, you may not need to include the rows that represent the subtotals generated by GROUP BY, but include only the total rows. This is where the GROUPING SETS extension of the GROUP BY clause may come in handy:

```
SELECT r.reg_name region, TO_CHAR(TO_DATE(EXTRACT(MONTH FROM (o.orddat
e)),'MM'),'Month') month, SUM(o.total) sales
FROM regions r, orders o
WHERE r.reg_id = o.regid
GROUP BY GROUPING SETS(r.reg_name, EXTRACT(MONTH FROM (o.orddate)));
```

This query should produce the following report:

```
REGION               MONTH       SALES
-------------------- ---------  ----------
North America                      17880
Europe                            6310.5
                     January        5240
                     February       5550
                     March       13400.5
```

You receive an interesting result when performing a partial GROUPING SET operation like the one shown next:

```
SELECT r.reg_name region, TO_CHAR(TO_DATE(EXTRACT(MONTH FROM (o.orddat
e)),'MM'),'Month') month, SUM(o.total) sales
FROM regions r, orders o
WHERE r.reg_id = o.regid
GROUP BY r.reg_name, GROUPING SETS(EXTRACT(MONTH FROM (o.orddate)));
```

This should give you the following results:

```
REGION                MONTH       SALES
-------------------   ---------   ----------
Europe                January         1480
Europe                February        1850
Europe                March         2980.5
North America         January         3760
North America         February        3700
North America         March          10420
```

It's interesting to note that the above report doesn't include summary rows—neither for each month nor for each region. Instead, it shows you all those subtotal rows generated by GROUP BY and excluded from the full GROUPING SET operation discussed earlier in this section. In this sense, a partial GROUPING SET operation is a reverse operation to the corresponding full one.

Ranking

Looking back to Chapter 1, you might recall the discussion on the problem of finding the top three salespersons, in the *Asking business questions using data-access tools* section. In that example, you used the RANK analytic SQL function to compute the rank of each salesperson, based on their sales.

Turning back to the data structures discussed in this chapter, you might, for example, compose a query that will compute a rank for each region, based on the sales figures. To better understand how ranking works, though, let's first look at the query that simply summarizes sales figures per region:

```
SELECT r.reg_name region, SUM(o.total) sales
FROM regions r, orders o
WHERE r.reg_id = o.regid
GROUP BY GROUPING SETS(r.reg_name);
```

Here is the output you should see:

```
REGION                SALES
-------------------   ----------
North America             17880
Europe                   6310.5
```

Now let's look at the query that will compute a sales rank for each region in ascending order:

```
SELECT r.reg_name region, SUM(o.total) sales, RANK() OVER (ORDER BY
SUM(o.total) ASC) rank
FROM regions r, orders o
WHERE r.reg_id = o.regid
GROUP BY GROUPING SETS(r.reg_name);
```

This time, the query results should look like this:

```
REGION                    SALES      RANK
-------------------- ---------- ----------
Europe                   6310.5          1
North America             17880          2
```

As you can see in the above rows, not only are region sales arranged in ascending order, but the rank column has also appeared. If you don't want to see the rank column, you might remove it from the select list and add the ORDER BY clause with the rank function, rewriting the query as follows:

```
SELECT r.reg_name region, SUM(o.total) sales
FROM regions r, orders o
WHERE r.reg_id = o.regid
GROUP BY GROUPING SETS(r.reg_name)
ORDER BY RANK() OVER (ORDER BY SUM(o.total) ASC);
```

This should produce the following output:

```
REGION                    SALES
-------------------- ----------
Europe                   6310.5
North America             17880
```

As you can see, a little trick of moving the rank function from the select list to the ORDER BY clause lets you exclude the ranking column from the output, keeping sales figures in the sales column arranged in ascending order.

Windowing

Windowing functions make up another important group of analytic SQL functions. The idea behind windowing functions is that they enable aggregate calculations to be made within a "sliding window" that may float down as you proceed through the result set. For example, you might want to include a sliding average column in the report containing total monthly sales. This column would contain the average sales for each row, based on the sales figures in the preceding, current, and following rows. Thus, the average for the January row will be calculated based on the value of the sales field in the January row, as well as the value of the sales field in the February row. In turn, the average for the February row will be determined using the sales field's values throughout all three rows. Finally, the average for the March row will be computed based on the sales for February and March.

The following diagram gives a graphical illustration of this example:

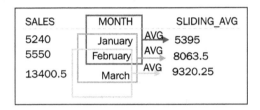

Let's first look at the query that simply calculates total monthly sales, which should look like this:

```
SELECT TO_CHAR(TO_DATE(EXTRACT(MONTH FROM (o.orddate)),'MM'),'Month')
month, SUM(o.total) sales
FROM   orders o
GROUP BY TO_CHAR(TO_DATE(EXTRACT(MONTH FROM (o.orddate)),'MM'),'Month
');
```

Here is the output:

```
MONTH          SALES
---------  ----------
January         5240
February        5550
March        13400.5
```

Now let's modify the query and define a "window" that will float down the above rows, calculating a value for the sliding_avg field. In the following query, note the use of the ROWS BETWEEN clause, and the keywords 1 PRECEDING and 1 FOLLOWING defining the parameters of the sliding window:

```
SELECT TO_CHAR(TO_DATE(EXTRACT(MONTH FROM (o.orddate)),'MM'),'Month')
month, SUM(o.total) sales,
AVG(SUM(o.total)) OVER (ORDER BY TO_CHAR(TO_DATE(EXTRACT(MONTH FROM
(o.orddate)),'MM'),'Month') ROWS BETWEEN 1 PRECEDING AND 1 FOLLOWING)
sliding_avg
FROM   orders o
GROUP BY TO_CHAR(TO_DATE(EXTRACT(MONTH FROM (o.orddate)),'MM'),'Month
');
```

The output should look like the following:

```
MONTH          SALES SLIDING_AVG
--------- ---------- -----------
February        5550        5395
January         5240      8063.5
March        13400.5     9320.25
```

Aside from the AVG function, you can apply the windowing technique using the other aggregate functions, such as SUM, MIN, and MAX.

Accessing external sources

When speaking about business reporting, it's important to note that there are some other native Oracle Database features, which, strictly speaking, are not considered among Business Intelligence ones, but can be a big help when it comes to collecting data from external sources. One of those great features is **XQuery**, which is natively available in Oracle Database starting with 10*g* Release 2.

Suppose you have to create a report showing data collected from both inside and outside the database. Say for example, that the data used in the report is stored in the hr.employees table as well as the bonuses.xml external document available via HTTP. As you might guess, the bonuses.xml document is supposed to contain information about bonuses to be given to some employees whose records can be found in the hr.employees database table.

The query used as the source for the report discussed here, might look like this:

```
SELECT XMLQuery(
'for $x in 1
  return (
  <EMPLOYEES> {for $i in ora:view("employees")/ROW,
  $j in $e/EMPS/EMP
  where $i/EMPLOYEE_ID = $j/EMPID
  return (<EMPLOYEE>
              <EMPID>{xs:string($i/EMPLOYEE_ID)}</EMPID>
              <NAME>{xs:string(fn:concat($i/FIRST_NAME, " ", $i/LAST_
NAME))}</NAME>
                  <BONUS>{xs:integer($j/BONUS)}</BONUS>
          </EMPLOYEE>)} </EMPLOYEES>)'
  PASSING xmlparse (document httpuritype
  ('http://localhost/samples/bonuses.xml').getCLOB()) as "e"
  RETURNING CONTENT).getStringVal() as RESULT FROM DUAL;
```

As you can see, this example assumes that the bonuses.xml document is available at http://localhost/samples/bonuses.xml. The source for this document might look like this:

```
<EMPS>
 <EMP>
    <EMPID>103</EMPID>
    <BONUS>2500</BONUS>
 </EMP>
 <EMP>
    <EMPID>104</EMPID>
    <BONUS>2000</BONUS>
 </EMP>
</EMPS>
```

With bonuses.xml shown previously, the query output should be as follows:

```
RESULT
-----------------------------------
<EMPLOYEES>
   <EMPLOYEE>
      <EMPID>103</EMPID>
      <NAME>Alexander Hunold</NAME>
      <BONUS>2500</BONUS>
   </EMPLOYEE>
   <EMPLOYEE>
      <EMPID>104</EMPID>
      <NAME>Bruce Ernst</NAME>
      <BONUS>2000</BONUS>
   </EMPLOYEE>
</EMPLOYEES>
```

Being part of an SQL statement, an XQuery query returns either XML or relational data that can be further processed within that SQL statement. In this particular example, the output is given in XML format, which is recognized by many reporting tools. For more information on Oracle XQuery, you can refer to the Oracle Documentation: *XML DB Developer's Guide*.

Discovering SQL in Discoverer

As mentioned earlier, visual Business Intelligence tools like Discoverer use SQL behind the scenes. Although you won't see any SQL code immediately after a visual IDE has been loaded, it's no more than 1 or 2 clicks away. In Discoverer Plus, for example, you can look at the SQL code behind a Discoverer item through the SQL Inspector, which you can launch by clicking the Tools\Show SQL menu. As an example, the SQL Inspector dialog containing the SQL behind the hr.employees item is shown in the following figure:

The following listing illustrates the SQL code behind the hr.employees Discoverer item in full:

```
SELECT O100032.EMPLOYEE_ID, O100032.FIRST_NAME, O100032.LAST_NAME,
O100032.EMAIL, O100032.PHONE_NUMBER, O100032.HIRE_DATE, O100032.
JOB_ID, O100032.MANAGER_ID, O100032.DEPARTMENT_ID, ( DECODE(O100032.
HIRE_DATE,NULL,TO_DATE(NULL,'MMDDYYYY'),TO_DATE(TO_CHAR(TRUNC(O100032.
HIRE_DATE,'YYYY'),'YYYY')||'01','YYYYMM')) ), ( DECODE(O100032.HIRE_
DATE,NULL,TO_DATE(NULL,'MMDDYYYY'),TO_DATE(TO_CHAR(TRUNC(O100032.
HIRE_DATE,'Q'),'MM')||'1900','MMYYYY')) ), ( DECODE(O100032.HIRE.
DATE,NULL,TO_DATE(NULL,'MMDDYYYY'),TO_DATE(TO_CHAR(TRUNC(O100032.
HIRE_DATE,'MM'),'MM')||'1900','MMYYYY')) ), ( DECODE(O100032.HIRE_
DATE,NULL,TO_DATE(NULL,'MMDDYYYY'),TO_DATE(TO_CHAR(TRUNC(O100032.HIRE_
```

```
DATE,'DD'),'DD')||'190001','DDYYYYMM')) ), SUM(O100032.COMMISSION_
PCT), SUM(O100032.SALARY)
FROM HR.EMPLOYEES O100032
GROUP BY O100032.EMPLOYEE_ID, O100032.FIRST_NAME, O100032.LAST_NAME,
O100032.EMAIL, O100032.PHONE_NUMBER, O100032.HIRE_DATE, O100032.
JOB_ID, O100032.MANAGER_ID, O100032.DEPARTMENT_ID, ( DECODE(O100032.
HIRE_DATE,NULL,TO_DATE(NULL,'MMDDYYYY'),TO_DATE(TO_CHAR(TRUNC(O100032.
HIRE_DATE,'YYYY'),'YYYY')||'01','YYYYMM')) ), ( DECODE(O100032.HIRE_
DATE,NULL,TO_DATE(NULL,'MMDDYYYY'),TO_DATE(TO_CHAR(TRUNC(O100032.
HIRE_DATE,'Q'),'MM')||'1900','MMYYYY')) ), ( DECODE(O100032.HIRE_
DATE,NULL,TO_DATE(NULL,'MMDDYYYY'),TO_DATE(TO_CHAR(TRUNC(O100032.
HIRE_DATE,'MM'),'MM')||'1900','MMYYYY')) ), ( DECODE(O100032.HIRE_
DATE,NULL,TO_DATE(NULL,'MMDDYYYY'),TO_DATE(TO_CHAR(TRUNC(O100032.HIRE_
DATE,'DD'),'DD')||'190001','DDYYYYMM')) )
;
```

Looking through the above SQL, you might notice how big the GROUP BY clause is in this automatically generated SELECT statement. As you might guess, this is due to a series of the SUM aggregate functions in the select list.

The above SELECT statement could include the ORDER BY clause as well, provided you selected a column, or columns, to sort when creating the item. You can also select columns to sort later with the help of the **Sort** dialog, available via the **Tools | Sort menu**.

Relational implementation of the dimensional model

You can regard this section as a prelude to covering the data warehousing Oracle Database feature, which will be discussed in detail later in this book.

Database structures behind an EUL

In the preceding section, you looked at the SQL code behind a Discoverer item. While that code represented the SELECT statement issued against a regular database table, there are some objects within Discoverer that require a set of associated objects in the underlying database to hold metadata.

Let's, for example, explore the database structures, which are implicitly defined upon creation of the HR EUL discussed in the "Post-installation tasks" section of the preceding chapter. For this, let's examine the hr/hr database schema upon which the HR EUL was created. To begin with, you can simply count the tables in the schema. To do this, connect to the database /as sysdba and then issue the following query:

```
SELECT count(*) FROM all_tables WHERE owner = 'HR';
```

The results produced should tell you what the number of tables that can currently be found in the `hr` database schema is:

```
COUNT(*)
----------
        55
```

The number of tables found here arouses a reasonable suspicion that it's too many for a demonstration schema. Continuing with your research, try to recall the date when you originally created the HR EUL. If you can recall it, you might issue the following query, reconnecting first as the `hr/hr` user:

 This example illustrates the use of the `user_objects` data dictionary view, through which you can find the creation date of a database schema's objects, such as tables, views, or stored procedures.

```
CONN hr/hr

SELECT object_name FROM user_objects WHERE object_type = 'TABLE' AND
TO_CHAR(created, 'DD-MON-YYYY') < '15-FEB-2010';
```

As you can see, this example assumes that you created the HR EUL on `15-FEB-2010`. The query should output the names of the 'native' `hr/hr` schema tables, which were created during the database installation; that is, at an earlier date.

As the query result should show, there are only seven such tables. Here they are:

```
REGIONS
COUNTRIES
LOCATIONS
DEPARTMENTS
JOBS
EMPLOYEES
JOB_HISTORY
```

What are the other 48 tables? As you might guess, the others are the EUL tables defined implicitly when creating the HR EUL. To look at the list of these EUL tables, you might modify the query above slightly, searching for the tables created on the date when the HR EUL was created:

```
SELECT object_name FROM user_objects WHERE object_type = 'TABLE' AND
TO_CHAR(created, 'DD-MON-YYYY') = '15-FEB-2010';
```

To save space, the output list is shortened here:

```
EUL5_ACCESS_PRIVS
EUL5_APP_PARAMS

. . .

EUL5_SUM_RFSH_SETS
EUL5_VERSIONS
```

These tables are related to each other with foreign key relationships, storing the EUL metadata. The following figure is a screenshot of the Model page in the Object Browser that is part of the Database Home Page. The Database Home Page comes with Oracle Database XE. Such a model visually illustrates the relationships of a database table. In this particular case, you can see the relationships that the EUL5_SUM_RFSH_SETS table establishes with the other EUL tables.

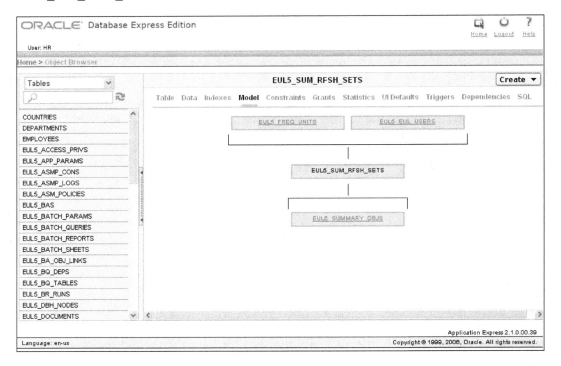

In the Object Browser shown here, if you move to the SQL page by clicking the SQL menu, you will see the CREATE TABLE and CREATE INDEX statements used to create the EUL5_SUM_RFSH_SETS table.

Summary

While the preceding chapters discussed Business Intelligence through the prism of visual Oracle Business Intelligence tools such as Discoverer, this chapter stepped aside and looked at how to use SQL, a native tool of Oracle Database, to get answers to business questions based on the database data. In particular, you looked at the advanced SQL features designed to summarize data, such as ROLLUP and CUBE extensions of the GROUP BY clause in SELECT statements.

Turning back to the Business Intelligence components from the Oracle Business Intelligence suite discussed in the preceding chapters, this chapter shed some light on how the metadata used by Discoverer is organized in the underlying Oracle database. In particular, you looked at the database structures behind EULs, which are needed in order to work with Discoverer.

The next chapter will come back to the discussion of the Oracle Business Intelligence suite, providing a detailed look at its components. Aside from Discoverer Plus, which is used in most of the examples in the previous chapters, you will look at the other intriguing Oracle Business Intelligence components, including Oracle Discoverer Viewer and Oracle Reports.

4
Analyzing Data and Creating Reports

In the previous chapter, you looked at some wonderful ways you can use SQL for business analysis and reporting. As you no doubt have realized, the only serious downside to this approach is that it requires you to manually compose SQL queries, which often is a time-consuming process, especially when it comes to answering complex business questions.

Using Oracle Business Intelligence components, you don't have to write SQL queries by hand. These clever tools hide the SQL complexities, allowing you to focus on the questions you have, without having to know or worry about how they're going to be implemented in SQL.

In this chapter, you will see the following Oracle Business Intelligence components in action:

- Oracle Discoverer Administrator
- Oracle Discoverer Plus
- Oracle Discoverer Viewer
- Oracle Reports Server
- Oracle Reports Builder

Analyzing and reporting with Discoverer

Some examples of using Discoverer were provided in the first two chapters, giving you some understanding of this Business Intelligence tool. The following sections take a closer look at Discoverer Plus, Discoverer Administrator, and Discoverer Viewer, explaining their features in more detail.

Preparing your working environment with Discoverer Administrator

Before you can start exploring the Discoverer Plus features, though, you need to create a working environment allowing you to look at those features by example. What you'll need is some data stored in the underlying database as well as an EUL making this data available for use in Discoverer. As for the database data, you will use the database already created in the preceding examples. If you've followed the instructions in the *Multidimensional data analysis with SQL* section of the previous chapter, you should have a database schema with the tables populated with data. If you haven't done it yet, do it now. Just to recap, you should have the usr/usr database schema and the salespersons, regions, and orders tables within it, populated with data.

The next step is to create an EUL that holds the metadata required to make the above data available for use in Discoverer. The simplest way to do this is using Discoverer Administrator.

As mentioned earlier, Discoverer Administrator comes with the Oracle Business Intelligence Tools suite, part of Oracle Application Server. However, if you're using Oracle Fusion Middleware, then Discoverer Administrator is shipped with the Portal, Forms, Reports, and Discoverer suite. In either case, though, Discoverer Administrator is a Windows-only tool.

What this means in practice is that, on platforms other than Windows, you have to use other tools to perform administration tasks. For example, to create an EUL, you can use the Discoverer EUL Command Line for Java tool available on either a Windows, UNIX, or Linux machine. For details on how to do this, refer to the Business Intelligence Discoverer EUL Command Line for Java User's Guide, which you can find using the Search Oracle Documentation feature on the Oracle Documentation page at http://www.oracle.com/technology/documentation/index.html.

The following are the steps of creating such an EUL with the help of Discoverer Administrator:

1. Launch SQLPlus, connecting to the database /as sysdba Then, issue the following GRANT command:

   ```
   GRANT CREATE VIEW TO usr;
   ```

2. After issuing the above command, you can quit SQLPlus.

3. Launch Discoverer Administrator by clicking **Start | Programs | Oracle Business Intelligence Tools-BIToolsHome1 | Oracle Discoverer Administrator**.

4. In the dialog, **Connect to Oracle Business Intelligence Discoverer Administrator**, enter the `usr/usr` username/password pair to connect to the database. In this dialog, you'll also need to enter the service name of the underlying database.

5. After you click **Connect**, Discoverer Administrator will check if you have access to at least one EUL. If not, it will ask you to create one now. Click **Yes**, which will open the **EUL Manager** dialog. If you have access to at least one EUL, you will be immediately connected to Discoverer Administrator. In that case, you can open the **EUL Manager** dialog by clicking the **Tools | EUL manager...** menu.

6. In the **EUL Manager** dialog, you should click the **Create an EUL ...** button to proceed to creating a new EUL. This will launch the Create EUL Wizard.

7. In the first step of the **Create EUL Wizard**, you can select a user from the list of database users. This can be done in the **Select User** dialog, which you can open by clicking the **Select ...** button in the wizard screen.

8. In the **Select User** dialog, click the **Go** button to see a list of all users available in the **Results** box. In this box, choose **usr** by double-clicking it.

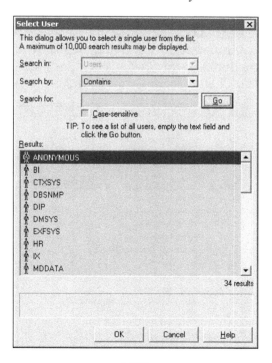

9. After a user has been selected, the **Finish** button in the **Create EUL Wizard** should become available. Click it to make Discoverer Administrator create the EUL. This process will continue behind the scenes and should take less than a minute. Once it's completed, you should see a message informing you about it.

10. Close the **EUL Manager** dialog by clicking **Close**.

After the above steps are completed, you have the usr EUL, which you can specify in the EUL field on the Discoverer Plus login page. However, the EUL created here is not the only metadata object you'll need to be able to work with the underlying database data in Discoverer Plus. What you also need to create is a business area, grouping the database data for analysis and reporting. If you recall, the concept of business area was briefly touched on the *Composing a Business Intelligence system* section in *Chapter 2, Introducing Oracle Business Intelligence*.

The following steps walk you through how to create a business area in Discoverer Administrator:

1. After closing the **EUL Manager** dialog in Discoverer Administrator, you should see the **Administration Tasklist** dialog shown in the following screenshot. If you don't see this dialog, click the **View | Tasklist** menu from the menu bar of Discoverer Administrator.

As you can see in the screenshot, the list of tasks you can accomplish with Discoverer Administrator is not limited only to creating business areas. Once a business area is created, you can perform tasks on its items such as creating joins, calculated items, and conditions. As you will learn a little later in this chapter, many of these tasks can be alternatively accomplished with Discoverer Plus when working with a business area.

2. In the **Administration Tasklist** dialog, click the **Create business areas** icon. This should launch the **Load Wizard** dialog shown in the following screenshot:

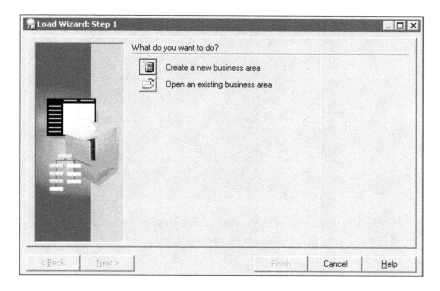

3. In **Load Wizard**, click the **Create a new business area** button. As a result, the **Next** button of the wizard should become available. Click the **Next** button to move on to the **Step 2** screen of the wizard.

4. In the **Step 2** screen of the wizard, choose the **usr** user in the **Select the users whose tables you want to load** box, and click **Next** to move on to the **Step 3** screen of the wizard.

5. In the **Step 3** screen of the wizard, in the **Available** box expand the **usr** list, select the **orders** item, and click the ▶ button to move **orders** to the **Selected** box. After that, click the **Next** button to proceed to the **Step 4** screen of the wizard.

6. In the **Step 4** screen of the wizard, click the **Next** button to move on to the last screen of the wizard.

7. In the **Step 5** screen of the wizard, enter `OrdersBusinessArea` in the **What do you want to name this business area?** box, and click the **Finish** button.

   As a result, a four-tab window called the **End User Layer USR** should appear:

8. Exploring the **End User Layer USR** window tabs, you can familiarize yourself with the structure of the newly created business area. For example, if you move on to the **Hierarchies** tab and expand the **OrdersBusinessArea** list, you should see how the **orddate** field inherited from the underlying **orders** table was shredded into the default date hierarchy:

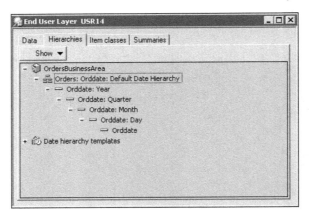

As you might guess, breaking a date item into a date hierarchy lets you drill in the data to view information in more detail.

Instead of the default date hierarchy shown in the figure, you might create a new one to apply to a date item. This can be done with the help of the **Hierarchy Wizard.** You can launch this wizard by clicking the **Insert | Hierarchy...** menu item.

For more details on creating and using date hierarchies, you can check Oracle Business Intelligence Discoverer Administration Guide. This document, like many others related to the Oracle Discoverer components, can be found on the Oracle Discoverer Documentation page at `http://www.oracle.com/ technology/documentation/discoverer.html`.

9. Now you can quit Discoverer Administrator by clicking the **File | Exit** menu item.

With an EUL and business area created as discussed in this section, you can move on and proceed to analyzing and reporting tasks with Discoverer Plus.

Exploring the Discoverer Plus IDE

Being a browser-based visual tool, Discoverer Plus has a powerful IDE simplifying the process of data analysis and reporting. In this section, you'll look at some of the most commonly used Discoverer Plus features, exploring them by example. In particular, you will do the following:

- Create a Discoverer workbook
- Compose a worksheet based on underlying database data
- Learn how the default date hierarchy is used
- Look at the underlying SQL code

The following discussion assumes you have created the usr EUL and OrdersBusinessArea business area discussed in the preceding section.

Before you can start exploring the Discoverer Plus IDE, you need to launch it. To do this, point your browser to the following URL:

```
http://yourhostname:7777/discoverer/plus
```

After a while, the Discoverer Plus IDE will be loaded and the first screen of the Workbook Wizard shown in the following screenshot should appear:

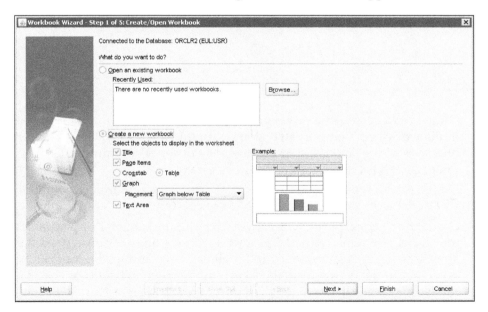

The Workbook Wizard shown previously will help you create a Discoverer workbook upon the underlying database data. In this particular example, you will create a workbook upon the `orders` table. The steps to creating a workbook are as follows:

1. On the first screen of the Workbook Wizard, leave all the settings at their defaults and click **Next** to move on the second screen.

2. On the second screen of the wizard shown in the following screenshot, select the `Orders` folder in the **Available** box and click the **>** button to move all the `Orders` folder's items to the **Selected** box. Then, click **Next** to move on to the next screen of the wizard.

3. On the third screen of the wizard, you should see the layout of information in the worksheet being created along with this workbook. Here, you can not only look at the layout but also change the order of columns as necessary. Then, click **Next** to proceed to the next screen.

4. On the fourth screen of the wizard, you can select a column or columns to sort in the worksheet. Then, click **Next** to continue.

5. On the fifth screen of the wizard, you can add a parameter or parameters to the worksheet being created. Parameters allow you to perform worksheet analysis by entering dynamic input values. For example, the user can be asked about the region to analyze each time the worksheet is opened or refreshed. Then, click **Finish** to complete the wizard.

6. Save the newly created workbook by the **File | Save as...** menu. This should open the **Save Workbook to Database** dialog. In this dialog, enter a name for the workbook, say, WorkbookOrders in the New name field, and then click **Save**.

Once the Workbook Wizard is completed, you should see the newly created workbook's worksheet with the data derived from the orders underlying table. The worksheet, along with the other components of the Discoverer Plus IDE, is shown in the following screenshot:

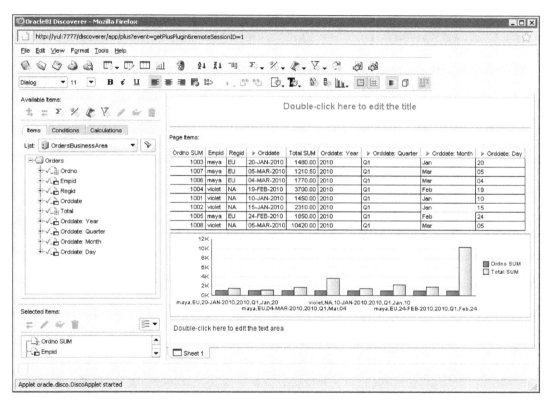

Looking through the worksheet, you might notice some new fields derived from orddate. These are as follows:

*   Year
*   Quarter
*   Month
*   Day

As you can see, these fields were automatically populated with the data, based on the values in the corresponding `orddate` field. You might be wondering how this sort of thing is possible. Although some may consider Discoverer Plus a black box, every hidden thing can be unveiled by looking at the underlying SQL code. Click **Tools | Show SQL...** to view the code behind the worksheet. This should look like the following:

```
SELECT O100022.EMPID,
O100022.REGID,
O100022.ORDDATE,
( DECODE(O100022.ORDDATE,NULL,TO_DATE(NULL,'MMDDYYYY'),TO_DATE(TO_
CHAR(TRUNC(O100022.ORDDATE,'YYYY'),'YYYY')||'01','YYYYMM')) ),
( DECODE(O100022.ORDDATE,NULL,TO_DATE(NULL,'MMDDYYYY'),TO_DATE(TO_
CHAR(TRUNC(O100022.ORDDATE,'Q'),'MM')||'1900','MMYYYY')) ),
( DECODE(O100022.ORDDATE,NULL,TO_DATE(NULL,'MMDDYYYY'),TO_DATE(TO_
CHAR(TRUNC(O100022.ORDDATE,'MM'),'MM')||'1900','MMYYYY')) ),
( DECODE(O100022.ORDDATE,NULL,TO_DATE(NULL,'MMDDYYYY'),TO_DATE(TO_
CHAR(TRUNC(O100022.ORDDATE,'DD'),'DD')||'190001','DDYYYYMM')) ),
SUM(O100022.TOTAL),
SUM(O100022.ORDNO)
FROM USR14.ORDERS O100022
GROUP BY O100022.EMPID, O100022.REGID, O100022.ORDDATE, (
DECODE(O100022.ORDDATE,NULL,TO_DATE(NULL,'MMDDYYYY'),TO_DATE(TO_
CHAR(TRUNC(O100022.ORDDATE,'YYYY'),'YYYY')||'01','YYYYMM')) ), (
DECODE(O100022.ORDDATE,NULL,TO_DATE(NULL,'MMDDYYYY'),TO_DATE(TO_
CHAR(TRUNC(O100022.ORDDATE,'Q'),'MM')||'1900','MMYYYY')) ), (
DECODE(O100022.ORDDATE,NULL,TO_DATE(NULL,'MMDDYYYY'),TO_DATE(TO_
CHAR(TRUNC(O100022.ORDDATE,'MM'),'MM')||'1900','MMYYYY')) ), (
DECODE(O100022.ORDDATE,NULL,TO_DATE(NULL,'MMDDYYYY'),TO_DATE(TO_
CHAR(TRUNC(O100022.ORDDATE,'DD'),'DD')||'190001','DDYYYYMM')) )
```

In the above SELECT statement, take a closer look at the DECODE functions in the select list. This should unveil what's under the date fields cover. In particular, you should see that each date field used here is derived from the `orddate` field of the underlying `orders` database table.

Continuing with exploring the worksheet, you might notice that the first column is called Ordno SUM. The above SELECT statement just confirms that the `ordno` column is selected as the SUM argument. What this means in practice is that you don't actually have the IDs of orders in this column but the sum of those IDs. The only reason why it seems you have the correct IDs in this particular example is that the GROUP BY clause in the query includes, among other fields, all the fields derived from `orddate`, thus grouping orders by the date of placing. And, as long as you don't have two or more orders placed on the same day, the SUM function in the select list does not actually aggregate anything. So, the data on the worksheet should look like this now:

Ordno SUM	Empid	Regid	Orddate	Total SUM	Year	Quarter	Month	Day
1003	maya	EU	20-JAN-2010	1480	2010	Q1	JAN	20
1007	maya	EU	05-MAR-2010	1210.5	2010	Q1	MAR	05
1006	maya	EU	04-MAR-2010	1770	2010	Q1	MAR	04
1004	violet	NA	19-FEB-2010	3700	2010	Q1	FEB	19
1001	violet	NA	10-JAN-2010	1450	2010	Q1	JAN	10
1002	violet	NA	15-JAN-2010	2310	2010	Q1	JAN	15
1005	maya	EU	24-FEB-2010	1850	2010	Q1	FEB	24
1008	violet	NA	05-MAR-2010	10420	2010	Q1	MAR	05

This won't be the case, though, should you insert a new order with a date already used in an existing order, specifying the same salesperson ID and the same region ID as well (this is because these fields are also included in the GROUP BY clause, as you might notice). For example, you might connect to the usr/usr database schema with SQLPlus and issue the following query:

```
INSERT INTO orders VALUES
(1010, 'violet', 'NA', '05-MAR-2010', 5310.00);

COMMIT;
```

Now, if you refresh the data on the worksheet by clicking the **Refresh** button on the Discoverer toolbar, you should see that the worksheet's contents have changed as follows:

Ordno SUM	Empid	Regid	Orddate	Total SUM	Year	Quarter	Month	Day
1003	maya	EU	20-JAN-2010	1480	2010	Q1	JAN	20
1007	maya	EU	05-MAR-2010	1210.5	2010	Q1	MAR	05
1006	maya	EU	04-MAR-2010	1770	2010	Q1	MAR	04
1004	violet	NA	19-FEB-2010	3700	2010	Q1	FEB	19
1001	violet	NA	10-JAN-2010	1450	2010	Q1	JAN	10
1002	violet	NA	15-JAN-2010	2310	2010	Q1	JAN	15
1005	maya	EU	24-FEB-2010	1850	2010	Q1	FEB	24
2018	**violet**	**NA**	**05-MAR-2010**	**15730**	**2010**	**Q1**	**MAR**	**05**

Needless to say, the value of the Ordno SUM field in the highlighted row is not what you might expect to find there. It's fairly obvious that summing up along an ID column is meaningless.

You might be asking yourself: how could that have happened? In fact, it can happen all too easily when building components like a business area or workbook with a wizard and leaving most wizard settings at their defaults (just what we did in the preceding examples). The problem is that, in Discoverer, a numeric field is aggregated with the SUM aggregate function by default.

> However, you might still leave wizard settings at their defaults and not find yourself in the situation described here. To avoid this sort of problem, it's always a good idea, when creating underlying database tables, to define ID columns as a character datatype such as VARCHAR2 rather than numeric. Sometimes, though, such design decisions may not depend on you. In such cases, you can step aside from the Discoverer defaults and turn down the SUM aggregation for the column of interest.

So, let's now remove the SUM aggregation from the ordno column, set on it by default. This can be done with the following steps:

1. In Discoverer Plus, move on to the **Available Items** pane, also known as Discoverer Item Navigator, and located on the left.

2. In the **Available Items** pane, expand the **Ordno** item by clicking the plus sign on the left.

3. In the list of aggregate functions shown under the **Ordno** item, right-click **SUM** marked with the √ sign. As a result, the **Available Items** pane should look like the following screenshot:

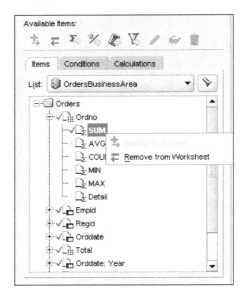

4. In the pop-up menu, select **Remove from Worksheet** to remove the **Ordno SUM** field from the worksheet.

   As you should see, the preceding step removed the entire **Ordno** column, not only the **SUM** aggregation. So, you now need to restore this column without the **SUM** aggregation, of course.

5. To add the **Ordno** column to the worksheet without aggregation, in the list of aggregate functions shown under the **Ordno** item, move down to **Detail** and right-click on it.

6. In the pop-up menu, select **Add to Worksheet** to add the **Ordno** column to the worksheet.

7. To save the change made, select the **File | Save** menu option.

After the above steps are completed, you should see one more row in the worksheet and the values in the `Ordno` column are correct throughout the entire result set:

Ordno	Empid	Regid	Orddate	Total SUM	Year	Quarter	Month	Day
1003	maya	EU	20-JAN-2010	1480	2010	Q1	JAN	20
1007	maya	EU	05-MAR-2010	1210.5	2010	Q1	MAR	05
1006	maya	EU	04-MAR-2010	1770	2010	Q1	MAR	04
1004	violet	NA	19-FEB-2010	3700	2010	Q1	FEB	19
1001	violet	NA	10-JAN-2010	1450	2010	Q1	JAN	10
1002	violet	NA	15-JAN-2010	2310	2010	Q1	JAN	15
1005	maya	EU	24-FEB-2010	1850	2010	Q1	FEB	24
1008	**violet**	**NA**	**05-MAR-2010**	**10420**	**2010**	**Q1**	**MAR**	**05**
1010	**violet**	**NA**	**05-MAR-2010**	**5310**	**2010**	**Q1**	**MAR**	**05**

As you can see, each row in the above worksheet represents an order. But what if you want to see order total aggregations per day? In this case, you'll have to remove the `Ordno` column from the worksheet. Once you've done it, the worksheet should look like this:

Empid	Regid	Orddate	Total SUM	Year	Quarter	Month	Day
maya	EU	20-JAN-2010	1480	2010	Q1	JAN	20
maya	EU	05-MAR-2010	1210.5	2010	Q1	MAR	05
maya	EU	04-MAR-2010	1770	2010	Q1	MAR	04
violet	NA	19-FEB-2010	3700	2010	Q1	FEB	19
violet	NA	10-JAN-2010	1450	2010	Q1	JAN	10
violet	NA	15-JAN-2010	2310	2010	Q1	JAN	15
maya	EU	24-FEB-2010	1850	2010	Q1	FEB	24
violet	**NA**	**05-MAR-2010**	**15730**	**2010**	**Q1**	**MAR**	**05**

As you can see in the previous worksheet, the `Total SUM` column shows order total aggregations at the date and region ID levels.

If you now look at the graph located after the worksheet, you should see that the `Ordno` column has disappeared from the diagram as well, thus providing a more meaningful graphical representation of the data on the worksheet (after all, there is no point in comparing the numbers behind order IDs):

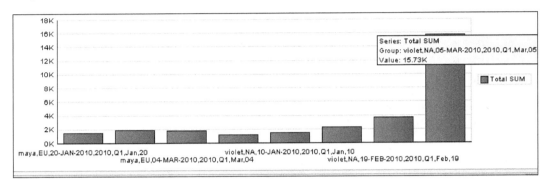

As you can see in the figure, the results are grouped by `Empid`, `Regid`, `Orddate`, `Year`, `Quarter`, `Month`, and `Day`. In this particular example, however, you might not go beyond `Regid` and `Day`. This is because, in this example, you have just two employees, each of whom is associated with a certain region (assuming you've populated the tables as discussed in *Chapter 3*). Moreover, there are no two orders placed by the same employee on the same day but in different months.

Maintaining a business-oriented view of relational data

Continuing with the example in the preceding section, it's interesting to note that you might still have the `Ordno` column in the worksheet and aggregate over the `Total SUM` column, summarizing totals at the date and region ID levels. So the worksheet's data would look like this:

```
Ordno Empid  Regid Orddate     Total SUM Year Quarter Month Day
-------------------------------------------------------------------
1006  maya   EU    04-MAR-2010 1770.00   2010 Q1      Mar   04
1007         EU    05-MAR-2010 1210.50   2010 Q1      Mar   05
1003         EU    20-JAN-2010 1480.00   2010 Q1      Jan   20
1005         EU    24-FEB-2010 1850.00   2010 Q1      Feb   24
             Sum: 6310.50
1008  violet NA    05-MAR-2010 10420.00  2010 Q1      Mar   05
1010         NA    05-MAR-2010 5310.00   2010 Q1      Mar
```

```
              Sum: 15730.00
1001          NA   10-JAN-2010   1450.00   2010 Q1      Jan   10
1002          NA   15-JAN-2010   2310.00   2010 Q1      Jan   15
1004          NA   19-FEB-2010   3700.00   2010 Q1      Feb   19
              Sum: 23190.00
```

Looking through this worksheet's data, you can notice that some new sum lines have appeared, summarizing totals at the date and region levels. To achieve this, you might perform the following steps:

1. In Discoverer Plus, select the **Tools | Totals...** menu. This should open the **Edit Worksheet** multi-tab dialog, on the **Select Items** tab, showing the **Calculations** tab of the **Available** pane. This should look like the following screenshot:

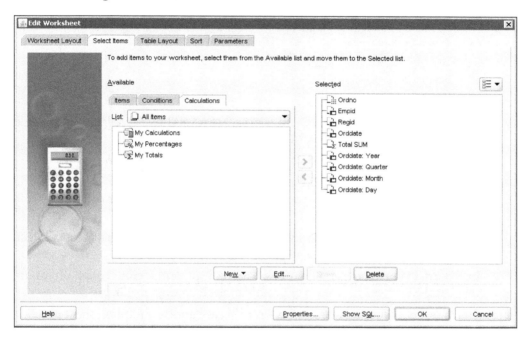

2. On the **Calculations** tab of the **Available** pane, right-click the **My Totals** item.

3. In the pop-up menu, select **New Total...** to open the **New Total** dialog shown next:

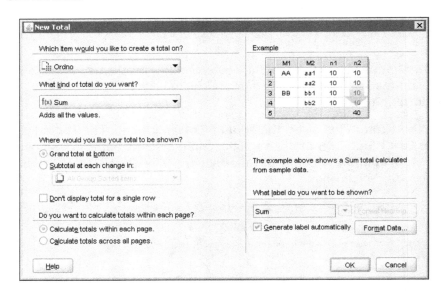

4. In the **Which item would you like to create a total on?** select list in the New Total dialog, select **Total SUM**.

5. In the What **kind of total do you want?** select list, select **Sum**.

6. In the **Where would you like your total to be shown?** group, select the **Subtotal at each change in:** radio button, and then select **Empid** in the select list below.

7. In the **Where would you like your total to be shown?** group, click to select the **Don't display total for a single row** checkbox.

8. In the **Edit Worksheet** dialog, click OK to complete the creation of a total on the **Total SUM** column with subtotals at each change in **Empid**.

    That's not it, though. Next, you need to create another total on the **Total SUM** column. This time, it should be with subtotals at each change in **Orderno**.

9. Repeat steps 2 through 8, selecting **Orddate** in the select list below the **Subtotal at each change in:** radio button.

    Once you're done, the **Calculations** tab of the **Available** pane in the **Edit Worksheet** dialog should look like this:

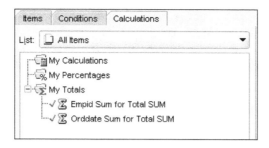

10. In the **Edit Worksheet** dialog, click **OK** to complete the operation.

11. To save the newly created totals such that they persist the current session, select the **File | Save** menu item.

Now if you look at the worksheet, you should see it contains a result set similar to the one shown in the listing at the beginning of the section.

In this section, you looked at an example of how you might add totals and subtotals to the worksheet. It's important to note that aside from these worksheet items, there are many other Discoverer features, which let you provide additional analysis to worksheets. In the following section, for example, you'll learn how to build a worksheet that will collect dynamic user input, updating the worksheet's data according to entered values.

Analyzing data

As mentioned above, Discoverer Plus has a lot to offer when it comes to providing analysis to worksheets. The most outstanding features will be discussed later in this book. For example, *Chapter 6, Pivoting Through Data*, will cover how to pivot worksheet items to arrange data for more effective analysis, and *Chapter 7, Drilling Data Up and Down*, will tell you how you might drill worksheet data up and down. This section explains how you might use Discoverer Plus parameters, building a worksheet that will update its data based on dynamic user input.

Suppose you want to add a dynamic parameter that would allow you to filter the worksheet data so that only the orders associated with a certain region are displayed. To do this, you might add a `Region` parameter through which you could specify the region ID upon opening or refreshing the worksheet.

The following steps will walk you through the process of creating such a `Region` parameter:

1. In the Discoverer Plus menu, select **Tools | Parameters...** to open the **Edit Worksheet** dialog at the **Parameters** tab.

2. On the **Parameters** tab of the **Edit Worksheet** dialog, click the **New…** button to open the **New Parameter** dialog shown in the next screenshot:

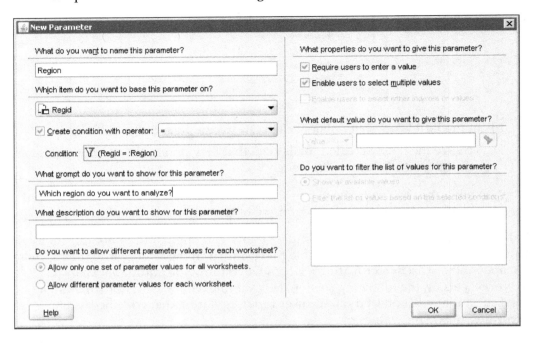

3. In the **New Parameter** dialog, type in **Region** in the **What do you want to name this parameter?** textbox.

4. In the **New Parameter** dialog, select **Regid** in the **Which item do you want to base this parameter on?** list.

5. In the New **Parameter** dialog, make sure that the **Create condition with operator:** checkbox is set and the operator in the list on the right is =.

6. In the **New Parameter** dialog, type in **Which region do you want to analyze?** in the **What prompt do you want to show for this parameter?** textbox.

7. In the **New Parameter** dialog, you can leave the other settings at their defaults and click OK to come back to the **Parameters** tab of the **Edit Worksheet** dialog.

8. On the **Parameters** tab of the **Edit Worksheet** dialog, in the Available parameters box you should see the **Regid** entry.

9. In the **Edit Worksheet** dialog, click **OK** to complete the creation of the parameter and come back to the worksheet.

10. Before the worksheet will be displayed, the **Edit Parameter Values** dialog shown next will be displayed, prompting you to enter the region ID:

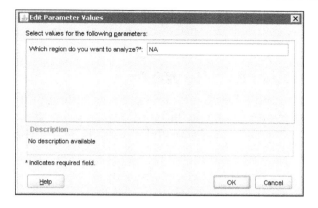

11. You can enter, for example, NA, and click **OK**. As a result, you will see the worksheet containing only the records with the NA region ID, as shown in the listing immediately after these steps.

12. To save the parameter, so that it persists the current session, select the **File | Save** menu item.

After performing the previous steps, you will have an active parameter associated with the worksheet, so that each time you open the worksheet or refresh it, you will be prompted to enter the value for this parameter. Once you enter it, the worksheet will be displayed, filtering records according to the entered value. These are the records you will see when entering NA as the value for the parameter:

```
Ordno Empid  Regid Orddate      Total SUM Year Quarter Month Day
----------------------------------------------------------------
1001  violet  NA    10-JAN-2010 1450.00  2010 Q1      Jan   10
1002          NA    15-JAN-2010 2310.00  2010 Q1      Jan   15
1004          NA    19-FEB-2010 3700.00  2010 Q1      Feb   19
1010          NA    05-MAR-2010 5310.00  2010 Q1      Mar   05
1008          NA                10420.00 2010 Q1      Mar   05
              Sum: 15730.00
              Sum: 23190.00
```

Now, if you click the **Refresh** button at the Discoverer toolbar and then enter EU when prompted, you should see that the record set shown on the worksheet has changed and looks as follows:

```
Ordno Empid  Regid Orddate      Total SUM Year Quarter Month Day
----------------------------------------------------------------
1003  maya    EU    20-JAN-2010 1480.00  2010 Q1      Jan   20
1005          EU    24-FEB-2010 1850.00  2010 Q1      Feb   24
1006          EU    04-MAR-2010 1770.00  2010 Q1      Mar   04
1007          EU    05-MAR-2010 1210.50  2010 Q1      Mar   05
              Sum: 6310.50
```

As you can see in both listings, the total items created as discussed earlier in this section are still active, summarizing filtered rows at the date and region levels.

Using Discoverer Viewer

Discoverer Viewer is another Discoverer component. Although it's much more lightweight than Discoverer Plus, you still might want to use it for analysis and reporting. The main advantage of Discoverer Viewer is its easy-to-use, intuitive user interface.

To launch Discoverer Viewer, point your browser to the following URL: `http://yourhostname:7777/discoverer/viewer`.

This should open the Discoverer Viewer login page, which looks similar to the Discoverer Plus login page and contains the same fields. If you recall, these fields were described in the end of the "Post-installation tasks" section in *Chapter 2* "Introducing Oracle Business Intelligence" earlier in this book.

After you've successfully connected to Discoverer Viewer, you should see the following window in your browser:

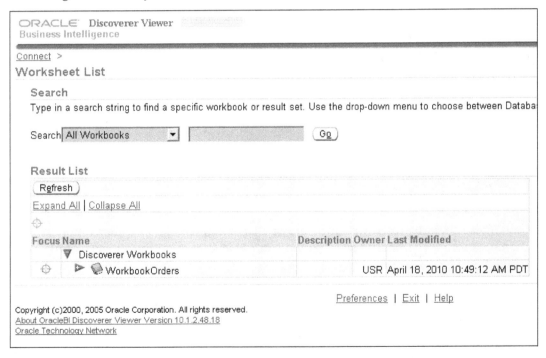

As you can see, Discoverer Viewer automatically found the workbook you have created in Discoverer Plus. You can open this workbook by clicking the + button on the left of the book's icon located in the `Result List` section.

As a result, you should see links to the book's worksheets. In this particular example, you should see a single link to the worksheet you worked with in the preceding examples. To open the worksheet, just click this link.

You may be surprised to find out that on the first screen you'll see you're asked to enter a value for the `Region` parameter you earlier created in Discoverer Plus. Here is what this screen will look like:

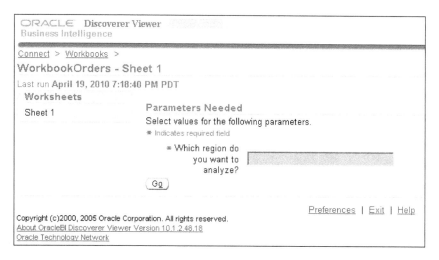

In the **Which region do you want to analyze?** textbox, enter a value, say, NA, and click **Go**. In return, Discoverer Viewer will generate an appropriate result set, displaying it in the **Table** section that should appear below. It's interesting to note the **Parameters you want to analyze?** textbox to change the result set shown in the worksheet.

Examining the worksheet's data, you might notice that not only the parameters created in Discoverer Plus remain in force, but the totals do too. The following screenshots illustrates what Discoverer Viewer should look like at this stage.

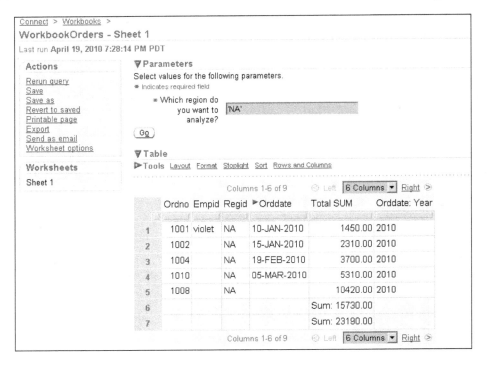

That's not the entire view, though. Just under the worksheet rows, you should see a graph similar to the one you saw in Discoverer Plus.

At the left, under the **Actions** heading, you can see the list of actions you can take. Among other options presented here, you can notice **Printable page**, which allows you to generate a printable PDF document of your worksheet. If you follow this link, you will be first directed to the ₚrintable Page Options page, on which you can set up print options. Once you're done, you can click **Printable PDF**. You'll be directed to the **PDF Ready** page, where you can follow the **Click to view or save** link to open the generated PDF document. The following figure illustrates what the generated PDF might look like:

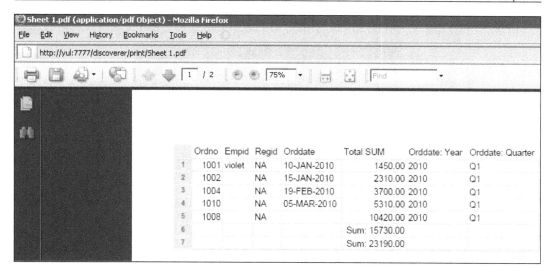

Now, you can save the document to disk or just send it to a printer, using standard Acrobat Reader tools.

Using Oracle Reports

Oracle Reports is another intriguing Oracle Business Intelligence component, which comes with the Oracle Business Intelligence suite. As its name implies, Oracle Reports is a reporting tool. It enables you to develop and deploy a wide range of reports against virtually any data source and then publish them in a variety of formats, including HTML, XML, and PDF.

Starting up the Reports Server

Oracle Reports uses Reports Server to listen for client requests and then processes them, generating requested reports or fetching the completed ones from the reports cache. Before you can make use of Reports Server, you have to start it up. This can be done with the following commands issued from an operating system prompt.

On Windows:

```
rwserver server= reports_server_name
```

On Linux, you would run the following command instead:

```
rwserver.sh server=reports_server_name
```

This should output the following dialog:

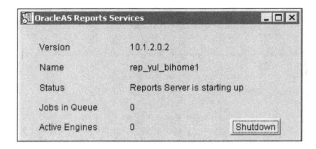

As you can see in the figure, you can always shut down the running server instance by clicking the **Shutdown** button.

Before you go any further, it's always a good idea to verify that the server is running and ready to process user requests. You can easily do this by pointing your browser to the following URL:

```
http://yourhostname:7777/reports/rwservlet/getserverinfo?server=rep_
server_name
```

As you might notice, even verifying the Reports Server is accomplished through the Reports Servlet. This is because you're doing it here using a web browser. The above should output the **Reports Server yourservername Information** page providing the information related to the server instance you just ran. This page is shown in the figure below:

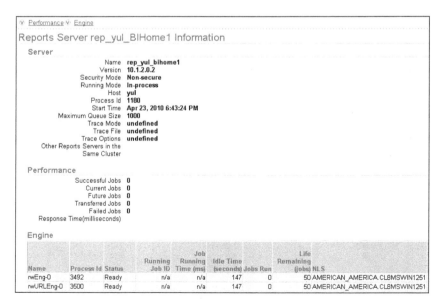

The most common problem you may face at this stage is failure of binding to the server. In this case, instead of the previous screen you would see the following error message:

```
REP-51002: Bind to Reports Server failed
```

The above often arises from a multicast communication problem that may require you to edit the $ORACLE_HOME/reports/conf/rwnetwork.cong file, increasing the timeout parameter of the multicast element from 1000 to, say, 60000, as follows:

```
<multicast channel="228.5.6.7" port="14021" timeout="60000"
retry="3"/>
```

Aside from Reports Server, it's also a good idea to verify Reports Servlet, another important component of Oracle Reports, which sits between either a web server or a J2EE Container and Reports Server, letting you run reports dynamically from a web browser. To verify that Reports Servlet is running, point your browser to the following URL:

```
http://yourhostname:7777/reports/rwservlet
```

The page it should generate is called **OracleAS Reports Services - Servlet Command Help** and contains information about the Reports Servlet commands.

Building reports with Reports Builder

Reports Builder is the Oracle Reports' development component. With the Reports Builder's Reports Wizard, you can easily build a report, which you can then deploy to Report Server.

This section will walk you through the process of building a simple report with the Reports Wizard. The report will be saved as a JSP document and then deployed to Reports Server. Here are the steps to follow:

1. Start Reports Builder by issuing the rwbuilder command from an operating system prompt. As an alternative, on Windows you could start it by selecting **Start | Programs | Oracle Business Intelligence Tools – BI ToolsHome1 | Reports Developer | Reports Builder**.

2. When Reports Builder has been loaded, you should see the **Welcome to Reports Builder** dialog shown in the figure below:

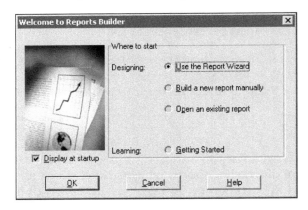

3. In the **Welcome to Reports Builder** dialog, make the **Use the Report Wizard** radio button is selected, and then click **OK**.

4. On the first screen of the Report Wizard called **Welcome to the Reports Wizard**, click **Next** to move on to the **Choose the type of layout you would like to generate** screen shown in the figure below:

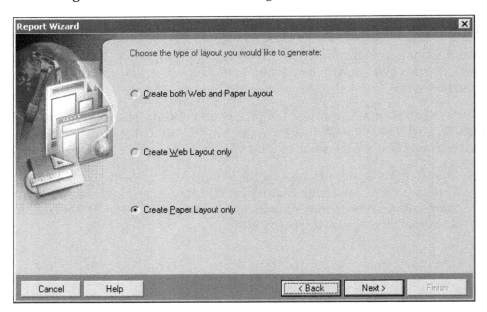

5. On the **Choose the type of layout you would like to generate** screen, select **Create Paper Layout only**, and click **Next**.

6. On the next screen of the wizard, you can specify the title for the report, say, **List of orders** in this particular example, and then select the report style. In this example, you might choose **Group Left**, so that you can group the report data later. Click **Next** to continue.

7. On the next screen called **Choose a data source type below**, select **SQL Query** and then click **Next**.

8. On the **Select data that you will use in your report** screen, click the **Query Builder...** button to open the Query Builder.

9. Before the Query Builder becomes available, you'll be asked to connect to the underlying database, entering the user name, password, and the database name as defined in the `tnsnames.ora` file.

10. After a connection is established, you will be asked to select tables in the **Select Data Tables** dialog. Select **orders** and click **Include** to include this table to the **Query** window of the Query Builder, and then click **Close** to close the **Select Data Tables** dialog.

11. In the **Query** window of the Query Builder, mark all the columns of the **orders** table as shown in the figure below, and then click **OK**.

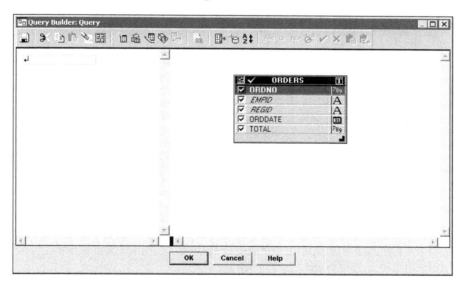

12. On the **Select data that you will use in your report** screen, click **Next**.

13. On the next screen called **Select the fields that you would like to designate as group fields...**, move the **regid** field from the **Available Fields** pane to the **Group Fields** pane. As a result, you should see the **regid** field under the **Level 1** node in the **Group Fields** pane.

14. In the **Group Fields** pane, select the **Level 1** node. Then, move the **orddate** field from the **Available Fields** pane to the **Group Fields** pane. As a result, the **orddate** field should appear in the **Group Fields** pane under the **Level 2** node, as shown in the figure below:

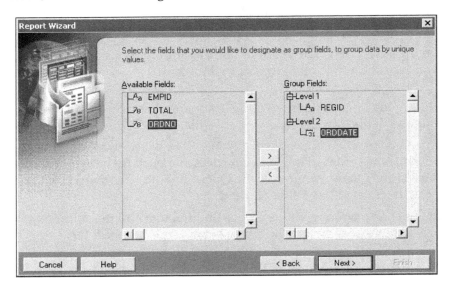

15. On the **Select the fields that you would like to designate as group fields...** screen, click **Next** to move on to the next screen.

16. On the **Select the fields that you would like to display in your report** screen, move all the available fields from the **Available Fields** pane to the **Displayed Fields** pane, and then click **Next** to continue.

17. On the **Select the fields for which you would like to calculate totals** screen, in the **Available Fields** pane select the **total** field and click the **Sum** button to move that field to the **Totals** pane. Then, click **Next** to continue.

18. On the **Modify the labels and widths for your fields and totals as desired** screen, you can leave the settings at their defaults, and click **Next**.

19. On the **Choose a template for your report** screen, leave the settings at their defaults and click **Next**.

20. On the final screen of the wizard, click **Finish** to complete creating of the report. As a result, the **Report Editor – Paper Design** window looking like the following figure will appear:

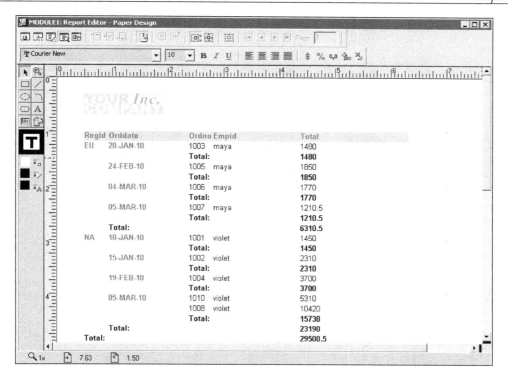

21. Close the **Report Editor – Paper Design** window.

22. In the **Object Navigator**, select the `MODULE1` node, and then select the **File | Save as...** menu of Reports Builder.

23. In the **Save** dialog, save the report as a JSP document to disk, naming it, say, `orders.jsp`.

Now that you have created the report, how can you run it against your Reports Server? To do this, just point your browser to the following URL:

```
http://yourhostname:7777/reports/rwservlet?report=c:/myreports/
orders.jsp&userid=usr/usr@orcl&destype=cache&desformat=pdf
```

Before moving on, let's take a close look at the parameters included in the above URL. As you might guess, the `report` parameter specifies the report source document to use, including the full path to this document. The `userid` parameter provides information about the underlying database containing the data for the report. And the `desformat` parameter specifies the format to use for the output.

As a result, the following PDF document should be generated, invoking Acrobat Reader within your browser:

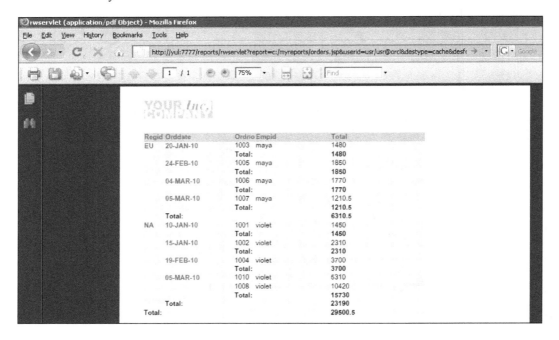

Now you can save the generated PDF document to disk, using standard Acrobat Reader means.

Summary

This chapter gave you some detailed examples of how you might use the Oracle Business Intelligence components for analysis and reporting. In particular, you looked at the Oracle Discoverer components, including Discoverer Administrator, Discoverer Plus, and Discoverer Viewer. Then, the chapter proceeded to another Oracle Business Intelligence component, Oracle Reports, explaining how you might use Reports Server and Reports Builder for building, deploying, and executing reports.

In the next chapter, you will look at how you can use the Oracle data warehousing feature for analysis and reporting. After a brief look at the architecture issues, the chapter will cover how to build a data warehouse, using a design tool such as Oracle Warehouse Builder.

5
Warehousing for Analysis and Reporting

In this chapter, you'll look at multidimensional data sources, often called warehouses, and their role in Business Intelligence. You will learn to build a data warehouse environment, thus structuring data for analysis.

As you will see in this chapter, data warehousing is a huge topic. Being an important Business Intelligence topic, warehousing deserves a book in its own right. A good example of such a book is the Packt's *Oracle Warehouse Builder 11g: Getting Started*. For details, you can visit the book's page on the Packt website at the following link: `https://www.packtpub.com/getting-started-with-oracle-warehouse-builder-11g/book`.

Although this chapter does not pretend to give a complete coverage of the warehousing topic, it provides a quick-paced guide covering how to build a data warehouse with Oracle Warehouse Builder. Following the instructions given in the chapter, you will learn how to perform the following:

- Obtaining and installing Oracle Warehouse Builder software
- Defining a data warehouse with Warehouse Builder
- Creating dimensions and cubes in a warehouse
- Getting data from warehouse sources into targets

Data organization in multidimensional data sources

As you might recall from the discussion in the *Aggregating Dimensional Data* section in *Chapter 1, Getting Business Information from Data,* a multidimensional data model is often used to perform complex analysis of historical data. For effective analysis, data should be organized along dimensions that can be then used for building cubes.

Dimensions included in a cube define its dimensionality, or in other words, its edges. For example, a cube can be organized along the Time, Store, and Product dimensions.

A dimension in turn is defined by a set of levels, each of which represents the level of data aggregation. For example, a store dimension may aggregate data at the following levels: Region, Country, State (Province), and Store.

Aside from links to dimensions, as you'll learn in this chapter, cubes contain measures representing usually numerical data that can be aggregated. Cost, quantity, and profit are good examples of measures.

Getting started with Oracle Warehouse Builder

Oracle Warehouse Builder offers a set of graphical user interfaces allowing you to implement a data store, either relational or dimensional, integrating and consolidating data from a variety of data sources. During building such a data store, also called a warehouse, you create a set of metadata objects within a workspace hosted on an Oracle database.

Oracle Warehouse Builder provides broad data integration facilities, making it a breeze to create Business Intelligence metadata for a wide range of data sources. You might want to use this powerful tool if, for example, you need to derive data from different database systems such as DB2, Informix, SQL Server, and Sybase, as well as flat files, XML, Web, and other disparate sources.

Once the data is derived, it will be automatically transformed into the data structures you have defined. It's interesting to note that you can use the Oracle Warehouse Builder's import facilities to make those data structures available to other Business Intelligence tools, such as Discoverer.

In the following sections, you'll learn how to install and then use Oracle Warehouse Builder. In particular, you will look at how to perform the following:

- Installing Oracle Warehouse Builder
- Creating a Warehouse Builder repository schema
- Creating a Warehouse Builder workspace
- Managing workspace users

Installing Oracle Warehouse Builder

Beginning in Oracle Database 11*g* Release 1, Warehouse Builder is automatically installed with the database. If you are using an older version of Oracle Database, you can install Warehouse Builder as a standalone software component.

The standalone Oracle Warehouse Builder software can be downloaded from the Oracle Warehouse Builder Downloads page at the following link:

```
http://www.oracle.com/technology/software/products/warehouse/index.html
```

It's interesting to note that you can download and install a newer version of Warehouse Builder on an older Oracle Database. For example, you might install Oracle Warehouse Builder 11*g* Standalone Software on Oracle Database 10*g*. Also, you might update an existing Warehouse Builder on a database even if Warehouse Builder is part of the database installation. For example, you can install Oracle Warehouse Builder 11*g* Release 2 Standalone Software on Oracle Database 10*g* Release 1 to take advantage of the new Warehouse Builder features.

The following steps assume that you have downloaded Oracle Warehouse Builder 11*g* Standalone Software and are installing it to be used with an existing installation of an Oracle database.

1. Launch **Oracle Universal Installer**, which will check your system and then display the Welcome screen.

2. On the Welcome screen of the Installer click **Next** to move on to the **Specify Home Details** screen.

3. On the **Specify Home Details** screen, specify a name for the installation and the full path where you want to install the product. Then, click **Next** to continue.

4. On the next screen of the Installer, you can specify your e-mail address that will be used to inform you about security issues. Then, click **Next** to continue.

5. After analyzing dependencies, the Installer should display the **Summary** screen, which might look like the following screenshot:

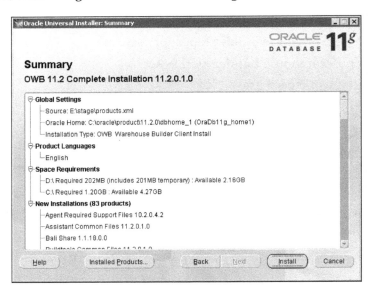

6. On the **Summary** screen, click the **Install** button to launch the installation process. On the **Install** screen of the Installer, you will see the process in detail. At the beginning of the installation process, the screen might look like the following screenshot:

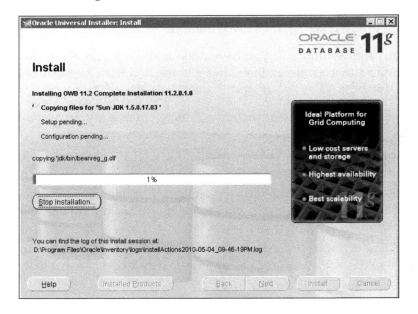

7. If the installation has been completed successfully, the Installer will display the following **End of Installation** screen:

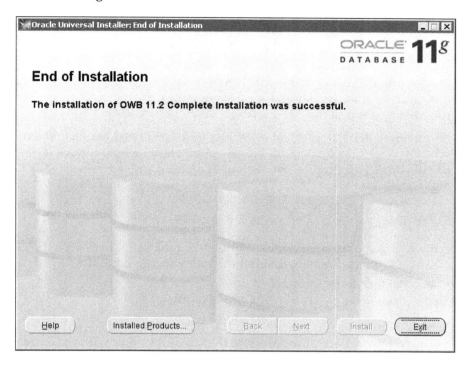

8. On the **End of Installation** screen, click **Exit** to exit the **Oracle Universal Installer**.

After the previous steps are completed, you have the Oracle Warehouse Builder software installed in your system. That's not it, though. The next step is creating a centralized Warehouse Builder repository in an Oracle database, also known as a workspace, to hold warehouse metadata objects.

Creating a Warehouse Builder repository schema

The following steps assume you're creating a Warehouse Builder repository on an Oracle Database 10*g*. If you're using an Oracle Database 11*g*, the first two steps are not required. The fact is, 11*g* has the OWBSYS schema by default.

1. Launch SQLPlus that was installed with your Oracle database, connecting to it as sysdba.

2. From within SQLPlus, run the `OWB_ORACLE_HOME/owb/UnifiedRepos/`
   `cat_owb.sql` script, using the `start` SQLPlus command. For example, the
   command to issue might look like the following:

   ```
   start c:\oracle\product\11.2.0\dbhome_1\owb\UnifiedRepos\cat_owb.
   sql
   ```

   As a result, you should see the OWBSYS schema is created. When prompted
   to enter the tablespace name for the newly created OWBSYS schema, enter
   USERS. After that, you should see a lot of tables, indexes, synonyms, and
   roles being created.

   As mentioned, on Oracle Database 11*g*, you don't need to create the OWBSYS
   schema as it exists by default. However, you still have to unlock it. You can
   do this through SQLPlus, connecting as `sysdba` and then issuing the following commands:

   ```
   ALTER USER OWBSYS ACCOUNT UNLOCK;
   ALTER USER OWBSYS IDENTIFIED BY owbsyspswd;
   ```

3. After the `cat_owb.sql` script is completed, make sure to unlock the newly
   created OWBSYS schema by issuing the following commands:

   ```
   ALTER USER OWBSYS ACCOUNT UNLOCK;
   ALTER USER OWBSYS IDENTIFIED BY owbsyspswd;
   ```

4. Next, you need to run the `OWB_ORACLE_HOME/owb/UnifiedRepos/reset_`
   `owbcc_home.sql` script to associate the Control Center with the correct OWB
   home. When prompted to enter **OWB Control Center Home**, you must enter
   the full path for the OWB Control Center install. For example, your path
   might look like the following:

   ```
   C:/oracle/product/11.2.0/dbhome_1
   ```

Creating a Warehouse Builder workspace

Once you have the OWBSYS schema installed and unlocked, the next step is to
launch and complete the **Repository Assistant** in order to install a Warehouse
Builder workspace.

1. On Windows, you can run it by selecting **Start | Programs | OWB_**
   ORACLE_HOME | Warehouse Builder | Administration | Repository
   Assistant. On a UNIX-like system, run the `./reposinst.sh` script that can
   be found in the `OWB112/owb/bin/unix` directory.

   As a result, the **Welcome** screen of the assistant shown next should appear:

2. On the **Welcome** screen of the assistant, click **Next** to continue.

3. On the **Database Information** screen, enter the information required to connect to the database. Then, click **Next** to continue.

4. On the **Choose Operation** screen, select **Manage Warehouse Builder workspaces**. Then, click **Next** to continue.

5. On the **Choose Workspace Operation** screen, select **Create a new Warehouse Builder workspace**. Then, click **Next** to continue.

6. On the **New or Existing User** screen, select **Create a workspace with a new user as workspace owner**. Then, click **Next** to continue.

7. On the **DBA Information** screen, enter the username and password of a database DBA. Then, click **Next** to continue.

8. On the **Enable Optional Features** screen, leave the settings at their defaults.

 It's OK to leave settings at their defaults if you're not going to production. If that's the case, though, be careful with what you choose, as raising a flag about optional features may mean extra license requirements.

Then, click **Next** to continue.

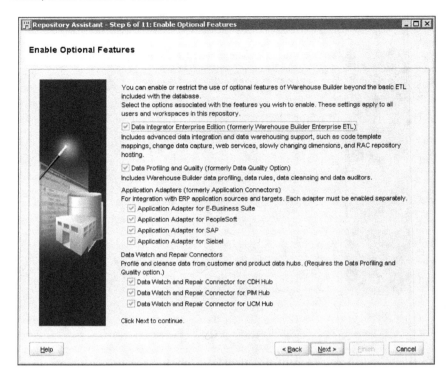

9. On the **Workspace Owner (New)** screen, enter a username and password for the database user that will be the workspace owner, as well as a name for the workspace. For example, you might enter **OWBUSER** for the database user and **myworkspace** for the workspace name. Then, click **Next** to continue.

10. On the **OWBSYS Information** screen, enter the OWBSYS's password. Then, click **Next** to continue.

11. On the **Select Tablespaces** screen, leave the settings at their defaults, and click **Next** to continue.

12 On the **Select Languages** screen, choose a language or languages of interest; for example, **English**. Then, click **Next** to continue.

13. On the **Workspace Users** screen, select the **usr** user and click **Next** to continue.

14. On the **Summary** screen, click **Finish** to complete the assistant and start the workspace installation.

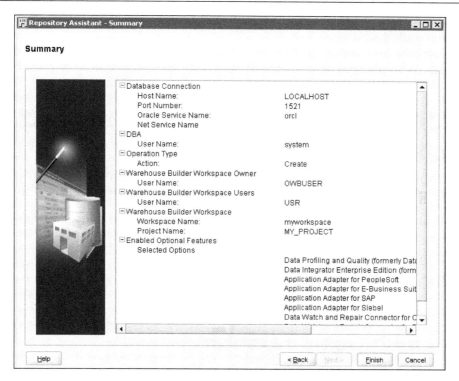

15. The installation process can take much time and its progress will be displayed in the following dialog:

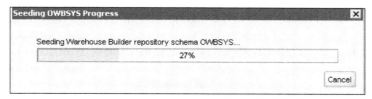

16. After it's been successfully completed, you should see the following dialog:

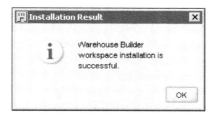

In the previous dialog, click **OK** to complete the installation.

Now that you have created a Warehouse Builder workspace, you can move on and log on to it with the Design Center, the primary graphical user interface of Oracle Warehouse Builder, with which you can design, deploy, and monitor your Business Intelligence systems.

Building dimensional data stores with Oracle Warehouse Builder

In the following sections, you'll learn how to build a sample warehouse with Oracle Warehouse Builder. In particular, you will learn how to perform the following:

- Working with Design Center, the primary tool of Warehouse Builder
- Creating a project for a warehouse
- Defining source and target modules
- Creating dimensions and cubes
- Populating dimensions and cubes with data

Launching Design Center

On Windows, to launch Design Center, you can select **Start | Programs | OWB_ ORACLE_HOME | Warehouse Builder | Design Center** from the Windows **Start** menu. On a Linux platform, run the following script OWB_ORACLE_HOME/owb/bin/ unix/owbclient.sh.

As a result, you should see the **Design Center Logon** dialog prompting for a workspace **User Name** and **Password** as well as the underlying database connection details. The dialog is shown in the following screenshot:

Looking at the previous screenshot, you may notice that **owbuser** is used as the
User Name here. According to the steps in the *Creating a Warehouse Builder workspace*
section earlier in this chapter, **owbuser** was created as the warehouse workspace
owner. Therefore, you can use this account to connect to Design Center.

Once you have provided the required information in the **Design Center Logon**
dialog and clicked **OK**, Design Center will be loaded. The Design Center IDE is
shown in the following screenshot:

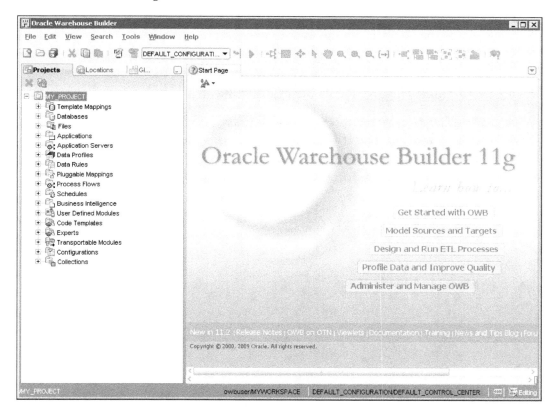

Now that you have loaded Design Center, the first thing you might want to do is
to create a project. However, it's not necessary as long as a default project named
MY_PROJECT is ready. Therefore, in this example let's use **MY_PROJECT**.

Proceeding with building a data warehouse, you will need to define the source
metadata describing the data structures upon which the warehouse is built and
the target structures representing your warehouse objects, such as dimensions
and cubes.

Defining source metadata

The first step in defining source metadata is to create a source module that will group the objects being imported from the underlying database.

Creating a source module

Here, you create an Oracle Database module that will represent an Oracle Database data source holding the data you're going to utilize. To do this, follow the next steps:

1. Move to the **Projects Navigator** and expand the MY_PROJECT\Databases node.

2. Under the MY_PROJECT\Databases node, right-click the **Or** item.

3. In the pop-up menu, select **New Oracle Module**.

4. On the **Create Module - Welcome** screen, just click **Next** to continue.

5. On the **Name and Description** screen, you can specify a name for the module being created or just leave a default name and click **Next** to continue.

6. On the **Connection Information** screen, click the **Edit...** button to specify the details of the connection.

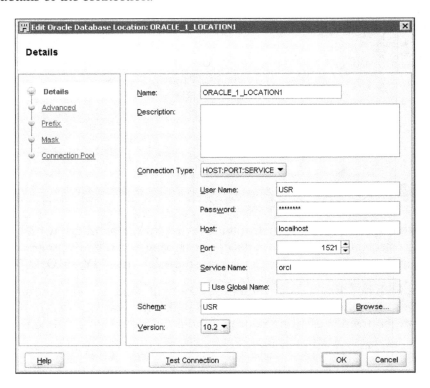

In the **Edit Oracle Database Location** dialog shown earlier, you must specify the connection information of the Oracle Database schema holding the data you want to use.

You might specify the usr/usr schema created and populated as discussed in *Chapter 3, Working with Database Data*, earlier in this book.

Before clicking the **OK** button, you can test the connection by clicking the **Test Connection** button. If the information you provided is correct, you should see a success message in the **Location Test Results** dialog.

Once you're done, click **OK** to submit the connection information and close the **Edit Oracle Database Location** dialog, returning to the **Connection Information** screen.

7. In the **Connection Information** screen, click the **Next** button to proceed to the **Summary** screen:

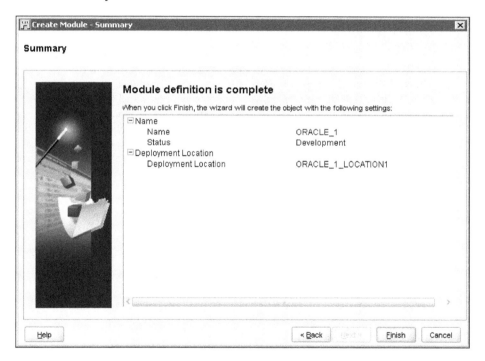

8. In the **Summary** screen, click **Finish** to complete the operation.

   As a result, the **ORACLE_1** module should appear under the MY_PROJECT\Databases\Oracle node in the **Projects Navigator**.

9. To save the changes you just made, select the **File | Save All** menu item of the Warehouse Builder.

Importing database objects

Now that you have created the module representing an Oracle database schema to be used as a data source, you need to import database objects stored in that schema. In particular, you will need to import the ORDERS, REGIONS, and SALESPERSONS tables created and populated with data as described in *Chapter 3, Working with Database Data*. Before proceeding to importing, though, let's create a few more tables in the source schema, which will be also used when building the dimensions and cube later in this chapter. Therefore, launch an SQLPlus session, connecting as usr/usr, and then issue the following SQL commands:

```
CREATE TABLE products(prodid NUMBER PRIMARY KEY,
prodname VARCHAR2(100), category VARCHAR2(30));
CREATE TABLE orderitems( ordno  NUMBER REFERENCES orders,
prodid NUMBER REFERENCES products, quantity NUMBER,
unitprice NUMBER(6,2),PRIMARY KEY (ordno, prodid));
```

> Alternatively, you could create the earlier tables with Design Center. For that, you could right-click the MY_PROJECT\Databases\Oracle\ ORACLE_1\Tables node in the **Projects Navigator**, and choose **New Table** in the pop-up menu. Once you're done with defining the columns and keys for a table, you need to generate and then deploy it to the database, using the Generate... and Deploy... menu commands respectively. These commands are available from the pop-up menu appearing when you right-click the newly created table node in the **Projects Navigator**. Before proceeding to deployment, though, make sure that the Control Center Service is running.

Once the tables have been created, you can populate them with data as follows:

```
INSERT INTO products VALUES(1110,'Orange juice','Beverages');
INSERT INTO products VALUES(1111,'Lemon juice','Beverages');
INSERT INTO products VALUES(1112,'shrimps','Seafood');
INSERT INTO products VALUES(1113,'mussels','Seafood');
INSERT INTO orderitems VALUES(1001, 1110, 36, 18.0);
INSERT INTO orderitems VALUES(1001, 1112, 5, 55.0);
INSERT INTO orderitems VALUES(1007, 1111, 30, 22.0);
INSERT INTO orderitems VALUES(1007, 1113, 10, 85.0);
COMMIT;
```

As we now have the ORDERITEMS table containing a unitprice field, we don't need the total column in the ORDERS table any more. Therefore, you can drop this column with the following statement:

```
ALTER TABLE orders DROP COLUMN total;
```

Now you can come back to your Design Center session and proceed to importing the database objects that will be then used in building the dimensions and cube. The following steps walk you through the process of importing:

1. Right-click the **ORACLE_1** module under the MY_PROJECT\Databases\ Oracle node in the **Projects Navigator**.

2. In the pop-up menu select **Import | Database Objects…**. As a result, the Welcome screen of the Import Metadata Wizard should appear.

3. On the Welcome screen, click **Next** to move on to the **Filter Information** as shown in the next screenshot:

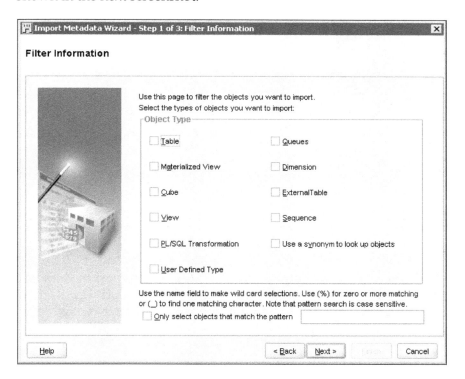

4. On the **Filter Information** screen, check the **Table** as **Object Type** and click **Next** to continue.

5. On the **Object Selection** screen, in the **Available** pane, expand the **Tables** node. Select the **ORDERITEMS** table, choose **All Levels** for importing dependencies, and then move **ORDERITEMS** to the **Selected** pane. The **ORDERS, PRODUCTS, REGIONS,** and **SALESPERSONS** tables will be also imported after you confirm it. As a result, the screen should look like the one shown next:

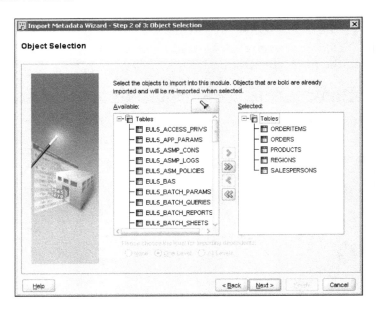

Click **Next** to continue.

6. On the **Summary and Import** screen, click **Finish** to start the importing process. Once it's completed, you should see the **Import Results** dialog providing you with the information about the actions that have been applied:

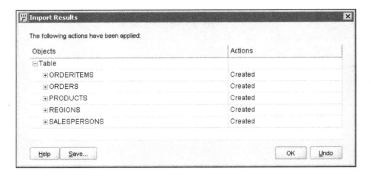

In the **Import Results**, click **OK** to complete the operation.

7. To save the results of importing, select the **File | Save All** menu item of the Warehouse Builder.

With that done, you have the source metadata imported and ready to use in your data warehouse.

Designing target structures

The next step is to design the target structures to which the source structures just defined will be mapped. Therefore, the target structures you will create here are the following:

- Target module
- Dimensions
- Cube

The following sections describe in detail how you might create these structures.

Creating a target module

As mentioned earlier, Warehouse Builder modules represent grouping mechanisms, combining target or source structures used in your solution. Like a source module, a target module defined in Warehouse Builder may correspond to a flat file or a database schema. It's recommended though that you use an Oracle Database schema as a target.

Although you might create such a module upon the OWBUSER Oracle database schema created as the workspace owner in the *Creating a Warehouse Builder workspace* section earlier in this chapter, you're encouraged to create and then use as a target another schema (not necessary the workspace owner's schema) in your Oracle database, thus achieving better flexibility.

The following steps walk you through the process of creating a target schema and then a target module upon that schema in Design Center:

1. In **Projects Navigator**, move on to the **Globals Navigator** tab.
2. On the **Globals Navigator** tab, expand the **Security** node.
3. Under the **Security** node, right-click the **Users** node and select **New User** in the pop-up menu to launch the **Create User** wizard.

Alternatively, you could create a new schema (user) in an Oracle Database through an SQL interface such as SQLPlus and then add it to Design Center. However, creating a database schema with Design Center, as discussed here, is easy.

4. On the Welcome screen of the wizard, click **Next** to continue.

5. On the **Select DB user to register** screen, click the **Create DB User...** button to open the **Create Database User** dialog.

6. In the **Create Database User** dialog, specify the system user password and then enter the information to create a new database user. For example, you might enter **owbtarget** as the username and **owbtargetpswd** as its password. Then, click **OK** to complete the operation.

7. In the **Selected Users** pane on the **Select DB user to register** screen, you should see the newly created **owbtarget** user. If so, click **Next** to continue.

8. On the **Check to create a location** screen, make sure that the **To Create a location** checkbox for the **owbtarget** user is checked, and then click **Next**.

9. On the **Summary** screen, click **Finish** to complete the operation.

   As a result, the **owbtarget** user should appear under the Security\Users node. The next step is to create a target module upon that user.

10. To create a target module, you can follow the steps in the *Creating a source module* section. This time, though, you won't need to define a location in the **Edit Oracle Database Location** dialog invoked by clicking the **Edit...** button on the **Connection Information** screen. Instead, just select the **OWBTARGET_LOCATION** in the **Location** select box.

    Once the module definition is complete, you should see module **ORACLE_2** under the MY_PROJECT\Databases\Oracle node in the **Projects Navigator** and don't forget to select the **File | Save All** menu item of the Warehouse Builder to save the changes you just made.

Creating dimensions

It's time now to proceed to implementing our dimensional design discussed in the *Data organization in multidimensional data sources* section earlier in this chapter.

The first step is to define the dimensions that will be then used in the cube. In other words, you need to define the dimensionality of the cube.

Creating a Time dimension

The following steps describe how to create a Time dimension:

1. On the **Projects** tab of the Projects Navigator, right-click node MY_PROJECT\ Databases\Oracle\ORACLE_2\Dimensions and select **New...** in the pop-up menu. As a result, the **New Gallery** dialog shown next should appear:

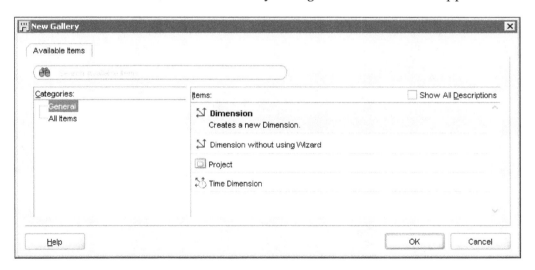

2. In the **New Gallery** dialog, select **Time Dimension** in the **Items** pane, and click **OK** to launch the **Create Time Dimension** wizard.

3. On the **Welcome** screen of the wizard, click **Next** to continue.

4. On the **Name and Description** screen, type in **TIME_DM** in the **Name** field, and then click **Next** to continue.

5. On the **Storage** screen, select **ROLAP** and click **Next** to continue.

6. On the **Data Generation** screen, specify the range of data you want to be stored in the time dimension. For example, you might specify **2009** in the **Start year** scroll box and **3** in the **Number of years** scroll box, as shown in the following screenshot. Also in this screen, select the **Calendar** radio button. Then, click **Next** to continue.

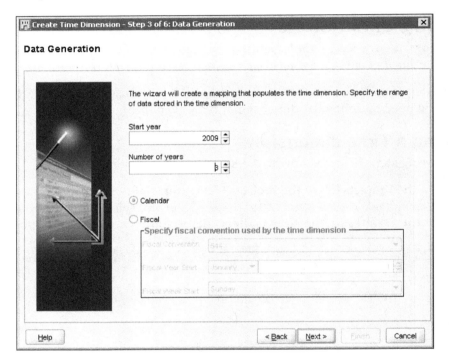

7. On the **Levels** screen, select **Normal Hierarchy** and check each element of the hierarchy, including the following:
   ○ Calendar **Year**
   ○ Calendar **Quarter**
   ○ Calendar **Month**
   ○ Day

Then, click **Next** to continue.

8. On the **Pre Create settings** screen, look through the settings of the dimension being created, and then click **Next** to start the process of dimension definition.

9. You should see the progress of this process on the **Time Dimension Progress Panel** screen. Once it's successfully complete, click **Next** to move on to the **Summary** screen.

10. On the **Summary** screen, click **Finish** to create the dimension.

11. Select the **File | Save All** menu item of the Warehouse Builder to save the dimension you just created.

Creating a Product dimension

Another dimension you'll need to create is a Product dimension that will also be used in the cube. There is no Product wizard in Warehouse Builder. Therefore, you can use the standard Create Dimension wizard, and the following steps describe how:

1. On the **Projects** tab of the **Projects Navigator**, right-click node MY_PROJECT\ Databases\Oracle\ORACLE_2\Dimensions and select **New Dimension** in the pop-up menu. As a result, the **Welcome** screen of the Create Dimension wizard should appear.

2. On the **Welcome** screen of the wizard, click **Next** to continue.

3. On the **Name and Description** screen, type in PRODUCT_DM in the **Name** field, and then click **Next** to continue.

4. On the **Storage Type** screen, select **ROLAP** and click **Next** to continue.

5. On the **Dimension Attributes** screen, you should leave the dimension attributes and their settings at their defaults and click **Next** to continue.

6. On the **Levels** screen, enter the following levels:
   ° Category
   ° Item

   Then, click **Next** to continue.

7. On the **Level Attributes** screen, make sure that all the level attributes for both the **Category** and **Item** levels are checked. Then, click **Next** to continue.

8. On the **Slowly Changing Dimension** screen, select **Do not keep history**, and then click **Next** to continue.

9. On the **Pre Create settings** screen, look through the settings and click **Next** to continue.

10. On the **Dimension Creation Progress** screen, click **Next** to move on to the **Summary** screen.

11. On the **Summary** screen, click **Finish** to complete the create dimension process.

12. Make sure to select the **File | Save All** menu item of the Warehouse Builder to save the dimension you just created.

Creating a Region dimension

To create a Region dimension, you can repeat the steps in the preceding section, specifying the following information:

- REGION_DM as the dimension name.
- Define the following levels:
  - ° Region
  - ° Employee

Creating a cube

You just completed creating dimensions. With that done, you can proceed to building a cube that will use them.

To complete this task with Warehouse Builder, you can use the Create Cube wizard. The following steps will walk you through the process of creating the cube:

1. On the **Projects** tab of the **Projects Navigator**, right-click node MY_PROJECT\Databases\Oracle\ORACLE_2\Cubes and select **New Cube** in the pop-up menu.

2. On the **Welcome** screen of the wizard, click **Next** to continue.

3. On the **Name and Description** screen, enter the cube name in the **Name** field — **SALES**. Then, click **Next** to continue.

4. On the **Storage Type** screen, select **ROLAP** and click **Next** to continue.

5. On the **Dimensions** screen, select all the available dimensions in the **Available Dimensions** pane and move them to the **Selected Dimensions** pane. Therefore, you should have the following dimensions:
   - ° PRODUCT_DM
   - ° REGION_DM
   - ° TIME_DM

   Then, click **Next** to continue.

6. On the **Measures** screen, enter the following measures:

   ○ **QUANTITY** with the **Data Type** as **NUMBER**

   ○ **AMOUNT** with the **Data Type** as **NUMBER**, with the
   Precision as **10**, and **Scale** as **2**

As a result, the screen should look like the following:

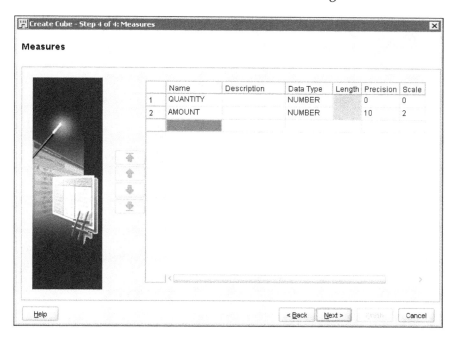

Then, click **Next** to continue.

7. On the **Summary** screen, look through the settings of the cube being created
   and click **Finish** to complete the operation.

8. Select the **File | Save All** menu item of the Warehouse Builder to save the
   cube you just created.

Building a staging table

Now that you've created a cube, how can you populate it with data? In other words,
how can you get the data from the source to the target? To accomplish this, you
might first create an intermediate table that will accumulate the data from the
source tables in a way so that it can be then easily transmitted to the cube.

Let's create table STAGE_TABLE in our target module ORACLE_2. Here are the steps to follow:

1. On the **Projects** tab of the **Projects Navigator**, right-click node MY_PROJECT\Databases\Oracle\ORACLE_2\Tables and select **New Table** in the pop-up menu.

2. In the **Create Table** dialog, enter **STAGE_TABLE** in the **Name** field, and then click **OK**. As a result, the Data Object Editor for the STAGE_TABLE table should appear.

3. Click the **Column** tab of the editor, and enter the following columns for the STAGE_TABLE table:

    ° SALES_QUANTITY NUMBER
    ° SALES_AMOUNT NUMBER(10,2)
    ° SALES_DATE DATE
    ° PRODUCTS_NAME VARCHAR2(100)
    ° PRODUCTS_CATEGORY VARCHAR2(30)
    ° REGIONS_NAME VARCHAR2(20)
    ° EMPS_NAME VARCHAR2(40)

4. Select the **File | Save All** menu item of the Warehouse Builder to save the table you just created.

Creating a staging mapping

The next step is to define a mapping that will be run to populate the STAGE_TABLE table, getting data from the source tables. The following steps walk you through the process of creating such a mapping:

1. On the **Projects** tab of the **Projects Navigator**, right-click the **Mappings** node under the target database module node MY_PROJECT\Databases\Oracle\ORACLE_2 and select **New Mapping** in the pop-up menu.

2. In the **Create Mapping** dialog, enter **SOURCE_STAGE_MAP** as the name for the mapping being created, and click **OK**. As a result, an empty canvas for the new mapping will be opened in the Mapping Editor.

3. Expand the `MY_PROJECT\Databases\Oracle\ORACLE_1\Tables` node containing the source tables, and then drag and drop all these tables to the **SOURCE_STAGE_MAP**'s mapping canvas in the Mapping Editor. So the Mapping Editor should look like the following screenshot:

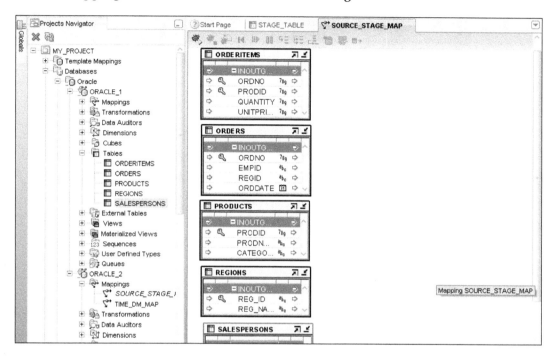

4. The next step is to drag and drop the target to the **SOURCE_STAGE_MAP**'s mapping canvas. Hence, expand the `MY_PROJECT\Databases\Oracle\ORACLE_2\Tables` node, and drag and drop the **STAGE_TABLE** table to the mapping canvas, on the right of the source tables.

Now that you have the source and target on the mapping canvas, your next step should be to connect them. In this example, this can be done with the help of the Joiner operator that you can pick up from the Component Palette of Warehouse Builder.

5.   In the Component Palette, find the Joiner operator and then drag and drop it to the mapping canvas between the source tables and the STAGE_TABLE table. Therefore, the mapping canvas now should look like the following screenshot:

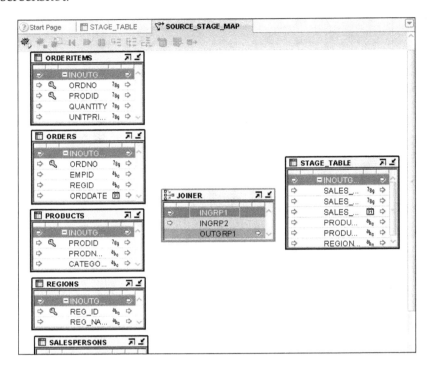

As you might notice, the Joiner operator contains only two input group operators by default. In this example, though, you'll need five of them, as you have five source tables.

6.   On the mapping canvas, right-click the Joiner operator and select **Open Details...** in the pop-up menu.

7.   In the **Joiner Editor** dialog, move on to the **Groups** tab. Here, rename two existing input groups and define three more input groups as follows:

   °   ORDERITEMS

   °   ORDERS

   °   PRODUCT

   °   REGIONS

   °   SALESPERSONS

Once you're done, click **OK** in the **Joiner Editor** dialog.

8. Now you can connect the source tables to the Joiner by dragging and dropping the output operator of the input output group of each source table to the corresponding input operator of the input group in the Joiner.

   Therefore, put the mouse pointer on the arrow on the right of the **INOUTGRP1** group in the **ORDERITEMS** table icon, press the left button of the mouse, and then move to the arrow to the left of the **ORDERITEMS** group of the Joiner, releasing the mouse button when you're there.

   As a result, you should see a set of connection arrows between the **ORDERITEMS** columns and these same columns that just appeared under the **ORDERITEMS** group in the Joiner.

9. Repeat step 8 for each source table.

   Once you're done, the mapping canvas should look like the following screenshot:

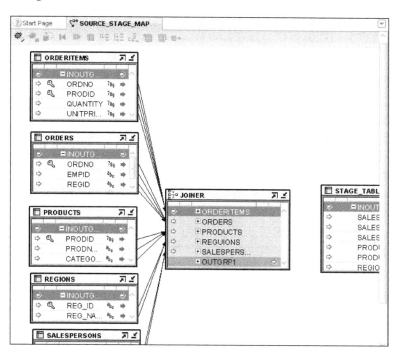

Now if you expand the **OUTGRP1** group in the Joiner, you should see 15 attributes under it, corresponding to the columns in the source tables. As attributes with the same names cannot appear within a single group, you will see **ordno** and **ordno_1**, and **prodid** and **prodid_1** here. As you might guess, these attributes correspond to the columns in the ORDERITEMS and ORDERS, and the ORDERITEMS and PRODUCTS tables respectively.

Before moving on, you need to define the join condition. Thankfully, Warehouse Builder does that work for us and all you need to do is to make sure that everything is correct here.

10. Click the Joiner header on the mapping canvas to select the Joiner. Then, go to the **Property Inspector**, and click the **...** button on the right of the **Join Condition** field to open the Expression Builder.

    The expression provided there should look like the following:

    ```
    ORDERS.EMPID = SALESPERSONS.EMP_ID AND ORDERS.REGID =
    REGIONS.REG_ID AND ORDERITEMS.PRODID =
    PRODUCTS.PRODID AND ORDERITEMS.ORDNO = ORDERS.ORDNO
    ```

    As you can see, the previous condition connects all the source tables to each other according to their foreign keys.

    Click **OK** in the **Expression Builder** dialog to close it.

 Joining is not the only step you have to perform when connecting the source tables with the target stage table. Another step is aggregation.

11. From the Component Palette, drag the **Aggregator** component and drop it into the mapping canvas between the **JOINER** and the **STAGE_TABLE** icons.

12. Connect the **OUTGRP1** group of the Joiner to the **INGRP1** group of the Aggregator. As a result, all the 15 attributes of the Joiner's **OUTGRP1** should appear under the Aggregator's **INGRP1** group.

 Another problem to solve is to cut off the time included in the ORDDATE attribute by default, so that only the date remains available. This can be done with the transformation operator available from the Component Palette.

13. Select the connection arrow between the **ORDDATE** attributes, and then delete it by clicking **Delete**.

14. From the Component Palette, drag the Transformation operator, dropping it into the mapping canvas between the **JOINER** and the **AGGREGATOR** icons. Before you can see it on the canvas, though, the **Add Transformation Operator** dialog should appear.

15. In the **Add Transformation Operator** dialog, select TRUNC under the **Date** package, and then click **OK**. As a result, the Transformation operator should appear on the canvas.

16. Connect the **ORDDATE** attribute of the Joiner's **OUTGRP1** to the **D** attribute under the **INGRP1** of the TRUNC.

17. Connect the **VALUE** attribute under the **RETURN** group in the TRUNC to the **ORDDATE** attribute under the Aggregator's **INGRP1**.

 So far you've worked with the input of the Aggregator; it's time now to move on and create its output attributes.

18. On the mapping canvas, click the header of the Aggregator to select the component so that its properties become available in the Property Inspector.

19. In the **Property Inspector**, click the **...** button to the right of the **Group By Clause** field to open the Expression Builder.

20. In the Expression Builder, build the following expression:

    INGRP1.PRODNAME, INGRP1.QUANTITY, INGRP1.UNITPRICE, INGRP1.
    CATEGORY, INGRP1.REG_NAME, INGRP1.EMP_NAME, INGRP1.ORDDATE

    Then, click **OK**. As a result, all the previously shown attributes should appear in the OUTGRP1 group of the Aggregator.

 If you recall, the stage table contains the sales_quantity and sales_amount aggregation columns. Therefore, you need to apply the SUM aggregation function to the QUANTITY and UNITPRICE output attributes of the Aggregator.

21. Right-click the **Aggregator** icon in the canvas and then select **Open Details...** in the pop-up menu.

22. In the **Aggregator Editor** dialog, move on to the **Output Attributes** tab, and change the name and expression for the **QUANTITY** and **UNITPRICE** attributes as follows:

    ° QUANTITY_SUM   SUM(INGRP1.QUANTITY)

    ° PRICE_SUM   SUM(INGRP1.UNITPRICE)

    Then, click **OK**.

23. The final step is to connect the attributes under the **OUTGRP1** group of the Aggregator to the corresponding attributes of the **STAGE_TABLE** table. Drag a connection arrow between each of the Aggregator's output attributes and the corresponding **STAGE_TABLES**'s attribute.

24. Select the **File | Save All** menu item of the Warehouse Builder to save the mapping you just created.

Loading the staging table with data

To load the STAGE_TABLE table with data, you need to execute the SOURCE_STAGE_ MAP mapping you just created. This can be done with the following steps:

1. On the **Projects** tab of the **Projects Navigator**, right-click the **STAGE_TABLE** node under MY_PROJECT\Databases\Oracle\ORACLE_2\Tables and select **Deploy...** in the pop-up menu. Make sure the deployment completed without errors.

2. On the **Projects** tab of the **Projects Navigator**, right-click the SOURCE_STAGE_ MAP node under MY_PROJECT\Databases\Oracle\ORACLE_2\Mappings and select **Start** in the pop-up menu. As a result, the **Confirm Deploy** dialog should appear.

3. In the **Confirm Deploy** dialog, click **OK** to confirm the deployment required before executing. The deployment process details will be shown to you in the **Job Details** window. Once the validation has been performed successfully, you'll be asked to click the **Start** button in the **Job Details** window to continue.

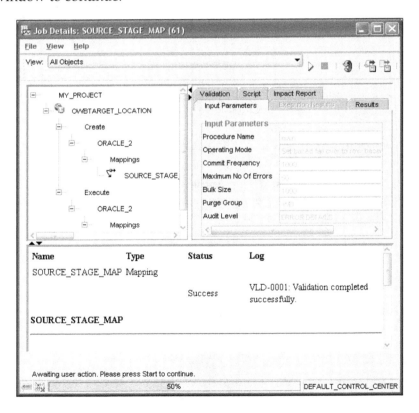

4. Once the execution process is completed successfully, you can look through the data loaded to the STAGE_TABLE table. For that, right-click the STAGE_TABLE node in the **Projects Navigator**, and then select **Data...** in the pop-up menu. Here is what you should see:

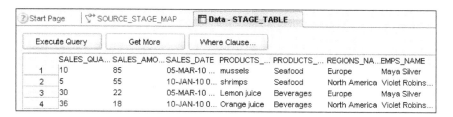

Creating mappings for loading data into dimensions

By now you have the STAGE_TABLE intermediate table loaded with the data. However, you still need to load the dimensions and cube created in the preceding sections of this chapter. Before you can do this, you need to create a mapping for each: PRODUCT_DM and REGION_DM dimensions.

Creating a product mapping

The following steps will walk you through the process of creating a mapping for the product dimension:

1. Select the **New Mapping** in the pop-up menu.

2. In the **Create Mapping** dialog, type in PRODUCT_MAP in the **Name** field, and click **OK**. As a result, an empty canvas for the new mapping will be opened in the Mapping Editor.

3. Expand the MY_PROJECT\Databases\Oracle\ORACLE_2\Tables node, and then drag and drop the STAGE_TABLE table to the PRODUCT_MAP's mapping canvas in the Mapping Editor.

4. Next, drag and drop the target to the PRODUCT_MAP's mapping canvas. This time it's going to be the PRODUCT_DM dimension. Therefore, expand the MY_PROJECT\Databases\Oracle\ORACLE_2\Dimensions node, and drag and drop PRODUCT_DM to the mapping canvas, on the right of the STAGE_TABLE table icon.

5. Connect the PRODUCTS_NAME attribute of the STAGE_TABLE to the NAME attribute under the ITEM group in the PRODUCT_DM, and then connect the PRODUCTS_NAME attribute to the DESCRIPTION attribute under the ITEM group.

6. Connect the PRODUCTS_CATEGORY attribute of the STAGE_TABLE to the NAME attribute under the CATEGORY group in the PRODUCT_DM, and then connect the **PRODUCTS_ CATEGORY** attribute to the DESCRIPTION attribute under the CATEGORY group.

7. Select the **File | Save All** menu item of the Warehouse Builder to save the mapping you just created.

Creating the REGION mapping

Now create the REGION_MAP mapping, repeating the steps in the preceding section. This time, you will need to connect:

- The REGIONS_NAME attribute of the STAGE_TABLE to the NAME attribute under the REGION group in the REGION_DM, and then to the DESCRIPTION attribute under the REGION group.

- The EMPS_NAME attribute of the STAGE_TABLE to the NAME attribute under the EMPLOYEE group in the REGION_DM, and then to the DESCRIPTION attribute under the EMPLOYEE group.

Creating a cube mapping

Similar to creating dimension mappings, you now need to create a cube mapping, connecting the STAGE_TABLE table to the SALES cube created as discussed in the *Creating a cube* section earlier in this chapter. Here is how you can create this mapping:

1. On the **Projects** tab of the **Projects Navigator**, right-click the **Mappings** node under the target database module node MY_PROJECT\Databases\Oracle\ ORACLE_2 and select **New Mapping** in the pop-up menu.

2. In the **Create Mapping** dialog, type in SALES_MAP in the **Name** field, and click **OK**. As a result, an empty canvas for the new mapping will be opened in the Mapping Editor.

3. Find the STAGE_TABLE table under the MY_PROJECT\Databases\Oracle\ ORACLE_2\Tables node, and then drag and drop it to the SALES_MAP's mapping canvas.

4. Drag and drop the target to the SALES_MAP's mapping canvas. This time it's going to be the SALES cube. Therefore, expand the MY_PROJECT\Databases\ Oracle\ORACLE_2\Cubes node, and drag and drop SALES to the mapping canvas, on the right of the STAGE_TABLE table icon.

5. Connect attributes in the INOUTGRP1 group of the STAGE_TABLE table to the corresponding attributes of the SALES cube as follows:

   ° SALES_QUANTITY | QUANTITY

   ° SALES_AMOUNT | AMOUNT

   ° SALES_DATE | TIME_DM_DAY_START_DATE

   ° PRODUCTS_NAME | PRODUCT_DM_NAME

   ° EMPS_NAME | REGION_DM_NAME

6. Select the **File | Save All** menu item of the Warehouse Builder to save the mapping you just created.

Deploying

Having created the cube mapping as discussed in the preceding section, you've completed the sample warehouse discussed here. The last steps are deploying and executing.

As you might guess, deploying is the process of implementation of the objects you've created in Warehouse Builder to the underlying database. Without this step, you won't be able to execute the mappings in order to load the data into the target objects. All the objects created in the ORACLE_2 target module, whether explicitly or implicitly, must be deployed. Therefore, you must deploy all the objects under the following nodes in the ORACLE_2 module, as they follow here:

- Sequences
- Tables
- Dimensions
- Cubes
- Mappings

To start deployment, you can right-click the object of interest and then select **Deploy...** in the pop-up menu.

Executing

Assuming you have successfully deployed all the objects mentioned in the preceding section, you can move on to the final stage: executing the mappings to get the data from the sources to the targets. In particular, you will load the dimensions and cube discussed in this chapter. To execute a mapping, right-click on it and then select **Start** from the pop-up menu. Execute the mappings in the following order:

1. SOURCE_STAGE_MAP

2. PRODUCT_MAP

3. REGION_MAP

4. TIME_DM_MAP

5. SALES_MAP

You might be tempted to look at the results of the execution, checking out the data in the underlying tables to which the dimensions and cube are linked. To do this, you do not need to leave the Design Center IDE. For example, to look at the contents of the PRODUCT_DM table containing the data loaded into the PRODUCT_DM dimension, you can right-click the table's node in the **Projects Navigator** and select **Data...** in the pop-up menu. As a result, the table's row-set should appear in the window on the right.

Summary

Of course, after reading this chapter, you may still have a lot of questions about warehousing. As you no doubt have realized, the purpose here was to give you a practical look at warehousing, without looking into details or concepts. Therefore, the chapter provided you just with quick-paced instructions on how you might build a warehouse with Oracle Warehouse Builder.

6
Pivoting Through Data

This chapter comes back to Oracle Discoverer, explaining how you can reorganize data on a worksheet for more effective analysis. In particular, you will learn to explore data relationships with pivoting.

Generally speaking, pivoting is a tool that allows you to look at the data from a different angle, rearranging worksheet items to meet your needs. For example, you may need to explore the sales by product or product category, rearranging the data so you can instantly see the sales figures for each product or category. In Discoverer, you can easily accomplish a pivoting operation using a drag and drop technique.

In this chapter, you will look at an example of pivoting and learn how to do the following:

- Create a crosstab worksheet in Discoverer Plus
- Rearrange data on a crosstab worksheet
- Pivot worksheet items using the drag-and-drop feature
- Create and use calculations

Making database data available for use in Discoverer

Before going any further, you need to create some metadata objects required to make the underlying database objects you're working with available for use in Discoverer. If you recall from *Chapter 4, Analyzing Data and Creating Reports*, the first step is to create an **EUL** (**End User Layer**) that contains metadata to access the database data and is designed to isolate you from database complexity.

In *Chapter 4*, you already created an EUL upon the usr/usr database schema. However, this underlying schema was modified in *Chapter 5, Warehousing for Analysis and Reporting*. So, you need to create a new EUL upon that schema. Since the process of creating an EUL was described in detail in Chapter 5, the following are only general steps:

1. Launch Discoverer Administrator.

2. In the dialog **Connect to Oracle Business Intelligence Discoverer Administrator**, enter the usr/usr username/password pair and the service name of the underlying database.

3. If you do not have access to at least one EUL, it will ask you to create one now. Otherwise, having connected to Discoverer Administrator, open the **EUL Manager** dialog by clicking the **Tools | EUL manager...** menu.

4. In the **EUL Manager** dialog, click the **Create an EUL ...** button to launch the Create EUL Wizard.

5. On the first step of the **Create EUL Wizard**, select the **usr** from the list of database users. In the **Select User** dialog, click the **Go** button to see a list of all users available in the **Results** box. In this box, choose **usr** by double-clicking it.

6. After selecting a user click the **Finish** button in the **Create EUL Wizard** to make Discoverer Administrator create the EUL.

7. Close the EUL Manager dialog by clicking **Close**.

As you might recall from Chapter 4, the next step is to create a business area in Discoverer Administrator:

1. After closing the EUL Manager dialog in Discoverer Administrator, the **Administration Tasklist** dialog should appear. If you don't see this dialog, click the **View | Tasklist** menu from the menu bar of Discoverer Administrator.

2. In the **Administration Tasklist** dialog, click the **Create business areas** icon.

3. In the **Load Wizard**, click the **Create a new business area** button. Then, click the **Next** button to move on to the **Step 2** screen of the wizard.

4. In the **Step 2** screen of the wizard, choose the **usr** user in the **Select the users whose tables you want to load** box, and click **Next** to continue.

5. In the **Step 3** screen of the wizard, in the **Available** box expand the **usr** list, select the orderitems, orders, products, regions, and salespersons items, and click the ▶ button to move them all to the Selected box. The result screen should look like this:

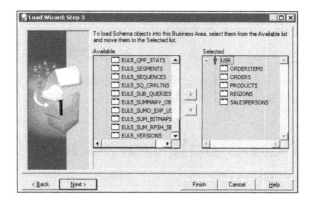

Then, click the **Next** button to continue.

 Unlike the example from *Chapter 4*, here you select more than one table, which would often be the case in a real-world situation.

6. In the **Step 4** screen of the wizard, click the **Next** button to move on to the last screen of the wizard.

7. In the **Step 5** screen of the wizard, enter SalesBusinessArea in the **What do you want to name this business area?** box, and click the **Finish** button.

8. As a result, a four tab window called the **End User Layer USR** should appear:

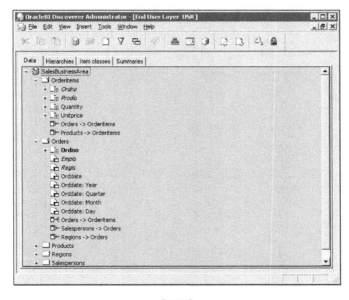

Note that the wizard automatically recognized the foreign key relationships between tables.

9. Quit Discoverer Administrator by clicking the **File | Exit** menu item.

The preceding steps complete creating the metadata required to make the underlying database objects available for use in Discoverer.

Creating a crosstab worksheet in Discoverer Plus

Now you can launch Discoverer Plus and connect to it as the `usr/usr` database user, specifying the `usr` EUL. As you already know, to launch Discoverer Plus, you can point your browser to the following URL:

```
http://yourhostname:7777/discoverer/plus
```

After Discoverer Plus IDE is loaded, the first screen you should see is the **Workbook Wizard** dialog. You should remember this wizard from the example in Chapter 4. The major difference from that example, though, is that this time you're creating a crosstab worksheet, not a table worksheet. The following steps will walk you through the process of creating a crosstab worksheet:

1. On the first screen of the wizard, select the **Crosstab** radio button, leaving all the other settings at their default:

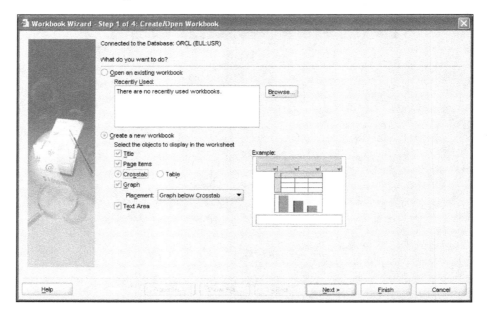

Click **Next** to continue.

2. On the **Select Items** screen of the wizard, you have to select the items you want to include in the workbook, moving them from the **Available** pane to the **Selected** pane.

    ° So, expand the **Orderitems\Quantity** node in the **Available** pane, and right-click the **Detail** item. In the pop-up menu, select **Add to Worksheet**.

    ° Do the same with the **Orderitems\Unitprice** node.

    ° Expand the **Orders** node in the **Available** pane, and right-click the **Empid** item. In the pop-up menu, select **Add to Worksheet**.

    ° Do the same with the **Orders\Orddate** item.

    ° Expand the **Products** node in the **Available** pane, and right-click the **Prodname** item. In the pop-up menu, select **Add to Worksheet**.

    ° Expand the **Salespersons** node in the **Available** pane, and right-click the **Name** item. In the pop-up menu, select **Add to Worksheet**.

    Once you're done, the **Select Items** screen of the wizard should look like the following:

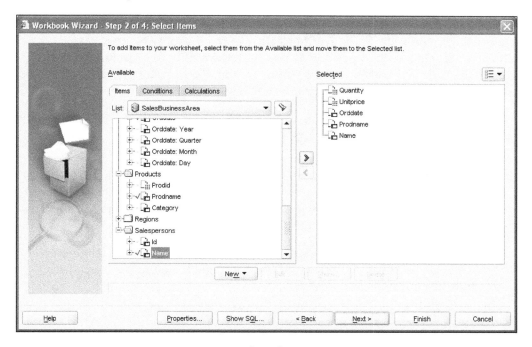

It's interesting to note that you must include not only those items that you want to use on the workbook's worksheets directly, but also those that will be used in calculations. Thus, in this particular example, you've included the Quantity and Unitprice items that will not appear on the worksheet but will be used in the Total SUM calculation.

Click **Next** to continue.

3. The first thing you should see upon transition to the next screen is the message box informing you that no data can be displayed in the crosstab. Just click **OK** to close it.

4. On the **Crosstab Layout** screen, you can change the worksheet's layout. For now, just click **Next** to continue. Close the message box that should pop up at this point again.

5. On the last screen of the wizard, click **Finish** to complete the creation of the workbook.

As a result, you should see an empty worksheet, just as Discoverer warned you.

Pivoting worksheet items

Obviously, the next step should be to populate the worksheet with data, so that you can then play with pivoting. Thinking about the data you would like to see on the worksheet, you most likely would like to see the dollar amount of operations performed during a certain period of time, with the ability to examine that data by salesperson, product, and/or product category. So, the first thing to take care of is to create a calculation determining this amount.

Creating a calculation

The product of the quantity and the unit price of the item in the order details gives you the dollar amount of the operation for that item — and, when summed up over the entire order for each item, it gives you the order total. Summing over all the orders gives you the total sales. Often, though, you need to aggregate sales figures across a certain time period at different levels.

Turning back to our example, let's create a calculation that will calculate the product of the Quantity and the Unitprice in the worksheet created in the preceding section. Here are the steps to follow:

1. In the **Item Navigator**, move to the **Calculations** tab.

2. On the **Calculations** tab, right-click the **My Calculations** item, and select `New Calculation...` in the pop-up menu.

3. In the **New Calculation** dialog, enter the name **Total SUM** for the calculation. Next, move the **Quantity** item from the **Selected Items** pane to the **Calculation** pane by double-clicking it and then clicking the **X** button located under the **Calculation** pane. Finally, double-click the **Unitprice** item in the **Selected Items** pane to complete the formula. By now, the **New Calculation** dialog should look like this:

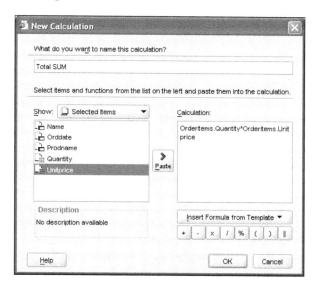

Once you're done with the formula, click **OK** to close the **New Calculation** dialog. As a result, the **Total SUM** calculation should appear under the **My Calculations** node on the **Calculations** tab. Also, the **Total SUM** column should appear in the worksheet layout.

Changing the worksheet layout

It's time now to work with the worksheet layout, so that it shows some data. To see more data on the worksheet, let's first add a couple of rows to the underlying database tables. So, connect to SQLPlus as `usr/usr` and issue the following statements:

```
INSERT INTO orders VALUES(1011, 'maya', 'EU', '10.01.10');
INSERT INTO orderitems VALUES(1011, 1111, 15, 22.0);
COMMIT;
```

Turn back now to the worksheet discussed here and follow the given steps to make it show some data:

1. First let's remove the `Quantity` and `Unitprice` columns from the worksheet. So, select the **Quantity** column and hit **Delete** to remove it from the layout. Do the same with the **Unitprice** column.

   At this point, the worksheet should look like the following one:

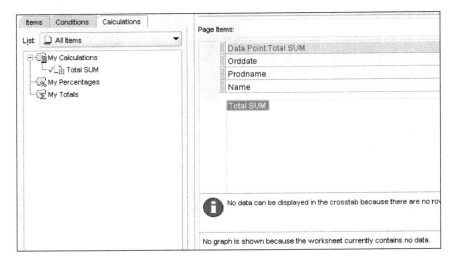

   As you can see in the screenshot, there are three items on the top axis and there is no left axis item.

 For details on axis items, refer to *Oracle Business Intelligence Discoverer Plus User's Guide.*

2. Let's move an item from the top axis to the left axis. Say, let's do that with the **Prodname** item, by dragging it to the left axis, just between the **Name** and **Orddate** items, as shown in the following screenshot:

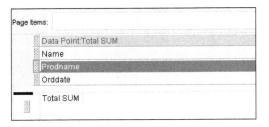

As a result of the previous operation, you should see that a dataset has appeared in the worksheet:

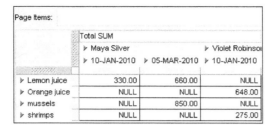

Page Items:			
	Total SUM		
	▷ Maya Silver		▷ Violet Robinso
	▷ 10-JAN-2010	▷ 05-MAR-2010	▷ 10-JAN-2010
▷ Lemon juice	330.00	660.00	NULL
▷ Orange juice	NULL	NULL	648.00
▷ mussels	NULL	850.00	NULL
▷ shrimps	NULL	NULL	275.00

Examining the worksheet data, you may notice that it's not properly formatted. In particular, dollar amounts presented here are not preceded by the dollar sign ($), as it might be expected by the user. So, it would be a good idea to format the data.

3. Right-click any cell on the worksheet and select **Format Data...** in the pop-up menu.

4. In the **Format Data** dialog, move to the **Number** tab and select the **Currency** category. Then, increase the **Decimal Places** to **2** as shown in the following screenshot:

Click **OK** to change the format and close the dialog. Now if you look at the worksheet, you should see that each number is followed by the $ sign and has two decimal places for cents.

5. Move the `Total SUM` item from the top axis to the left axis. The result should look like this:

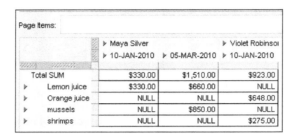

As you can see, the worksheet now aggregates the sales figures grouped by product for each date across salespersons.

The previous worksheet does not look detailed because you have just a few rows in each of the underlying tables. In practice, though, with thousands of records in the `orders` table alone, aggregating the data at the date level would result in a very multicolumn worksheet, unless you narrow down the allowed date range to just a few days. So, we often need to aggregate data at the month or quarter level.

Pivoting using the drag-and-drop feature

In the preceding section, you've built a worksheet, organizing the data at each axis at two levels. In particular, the data on the top level has been organized at the salesperson and date levels, and on the left axis at the total sum and product levels.

Now, suppose you want to look at the data from another angle, moving the **total sum** item to the top axis and the **Name** item to the left axis. This can be easily done with the drag-and-drop feature in the way you did in the preceding section. The resulting worksheet should look like the following screenshot:

Page Items:		
	Total SUM	
	▶ 10-JAN-2010	▶ 05-MAR-2010
▶ maya	$330.00	$1,510.00
▶ Lemon juice	$330.00	$660.00
▶ mussels	NULL	$850.00
▶ violet	$923.00	NULL
▶ Orange juice	$648.00	NULL
▶ shrimps	$275.00	NULL

Comparing this with the preceding screenshot, you might notice the figures in the worksheet have remained the same but their order has changed. No surprises here — this is simply a different perspective on the same dataset.

Suppose now you want to sum up the figures in the columns in the worksheet to see the total sales for each date. To do this, follow the given steps:

1. Go to the **Calculations** tab in the Item Navigator. Once there, right-click the **My Totals** item and select **New Total…**.

2. In the **New Total** dialog, select the **Total SUM** in the **Which data point would you like to create a total on** select box.

3. In the **New Total** dialog, select the **SUM** in the **What kind of total do you want** select box. The dialog should now look like the following screenshot:

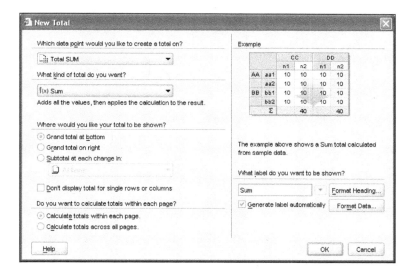

Then, click **OK** to create a new total and close the dialog. The worksheet should now look like this:

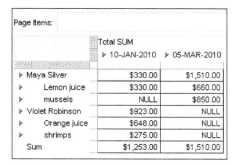

Summary

In this chapter, you looked at pivoting. You saw how easy it is to change a crosstab worksheet's layout with the help of the drag-and-drop feature of Discoverer Plus. The ability to pivot through data enables you to explore data relationships more efficiently, thus allowing for more effective analysis.

Continuing with the topic of reorganizing worksheet data for effective analysis, the next chapter will cover how you might drill data up and down.

7
Drilling Data Up and Down

Pivoting discussed in the preceding chapter is not the only technique that allows you to rearrange data on worksheets to answer the business questions you need to get answered. In Oracle Discoverer, you can also use drilling to analyze data, getting a new angle on the data you're dealing with.

There are several ways supported by Discoverer in which you can accomplish drilling. For example, you can drill data down to see more detailed information for a certain product. Or, on the contrary, you may need to view data at a higher level, drilling data up from products to categories. Another example is drilling to a related item, allowing you to add a related item that is not currently in the worksheet but can be found in a folder used by the worksheet.

This chapter will walk you through the simple steps required to drill data on Discoverer worksheets. With the help of many examples, this chapter will introduce you to the following:

- Navigating a Discoverer worksheet data with drilling
- Drilling up and down
- Drilling to a related worksheet item
- Drilling from a worksheet graph

What is drilling?

In terms of Oracle Discoverer, drilling is a technique that enables you to quickly navigate through worksheet data, finding the answers to the questions facing your business. As mentioned, depending on your needs, you can use drilling to view the data you're working with in deeper detail or, in contrast, drill it up to a higher level. The drilling to detail technique enables you to look at the values making up a particular summary value. Also, you can drill to related items, adding related information that is not currently included in the worksheet.

So, Discoverer supports a set of drilling tools, including the following:

- Drilling up and down
- Drilling to a related item
- Drilling to detail
- Drilling out

The following sections cover the above tools in detail, providing examples on how you might use them.

Drilling to a related item

Let's begin with a discussion on how to drill to a related item, adding the detailed information for a certain item. As usual, this is best understood by example. Turning back to the example at the end of the preceding chapter (the one discussed in the *Pivoting using the drag-and-drop feature* section), suppose you want to drill from the Maya Silver item, which can be found on the left axis of the worksheet, to the Orddate:Day item. Here are the steps to follow:

1. Let's first create a copy of the worksheet to work with in this example. To do this, move to the worksheet discussed in the preceding example and select the **Edit | Duplicate Worksheet | As Crosstab** menu of Discoverer.

2. In the **Duplicate as Crosstab** dialog, just click **OK**. As a result a copied worksheet should appear in the workbook.

3. On the worksheet, right-click the **Maya Silver** item and select **Drill...** in the pop-up menu:

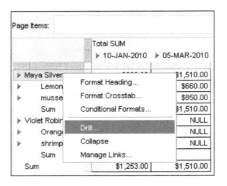

As a result, the **Drill** dialog should appear.

4. In the **Drill** dialog, select **Drill to a Related Item** in the **Where do you want to drill to?** select box and then choose the **Orddate:Day** item, as shown in the following screenshot:

5. Then, click **OK** to close the dialog and rearrange the data on the worksheet. The reorganized worksheet should now look like the following one:

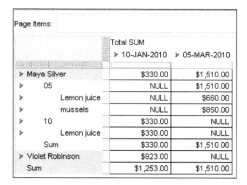

As you can see, this shows the **Maya Silver** item broken down into day sales per product.

Now suppose you want to see a more detailed view of the **Maya Silver** item and break it out further into product category.

6. Right-click the **Maya Silver** item and select **Drill…** in the pop-up menu. In the **Drill** dialog, select **Drill to a Related Item** in the where do you want to drill to? select box and then choose the **Category** item. Next, click **OK**.

The resulting worksheet should look now like this:

Page Items:			Total SUM	
			▸ 10-JAN-2010	▸ 05-MAR-2010
▸ Maya Silver			$330.00	$1,510.00
▸	Beverages		$330.00	$660.00
▸	05		NULL	$660.00
▸		Lemon juice	NULL	$660.00
▸	10		$330.00	NULL
▸		Lemon juice	$330.00	NULL
▸	Seafood		NULL	$850.00
▸	05		NULL	$850.00
▸		mussels	NULL	$850.00
	Sum		$330.00	$1,510.00
▸ Violet Robinson			$923.00	NULL
	Sum		$1,253.00	$1,510.00

As you can see, the result of the drilling operations you just performed is that you can see the dollar amount for Maya Silver detailed by category, by day, by product.

You may be asking yourself if it's possible to change the order in which the Maya Silver record is detailed. Say, you want to see it detailed in the following order: by day, by category, and finally by product. The answer is sure.

7. On the left axis of the worksheet, drag the `Orddate:Day` item (the third from the left) to the second position within the same left axis, just before the **Category** item, as shown in the following screenshot:

Page Items:			Total SUM	
			▸ 10-JAN-2010	▸ 05-MAR-2010
▸ M⟨⟩Silver			$330.00	$1,510.00
▸	Beverages		$330.00	$660.00
▸	05		NULL	$660.00
▸		Lemon juice	NULL	$660.00
▸	10		$330.00	NULL
▸		Lemon juice	$330.00	NULL
▸	Seafood		NULL	$850.00
▸	05		NULL	$850.00
▸		mussels	NULL	$850.00
	Sum		$330.00	$1,510.00
▸ Violet Robinson			$923.00	NULL
	Sum		$1,253.00	$1,510.00

As a result, you should see that the data on the worksheet has been rearranged as shown in the following screenshot:

Page Items:		Total SUM	
		▶ 10-JAN-2010	▶ 05-MAR-2010
▶ Maya Silver		$330.00	$1,510.00
▶ 05		NULL	$1,510.00
▶	Beverages	NULL	$660.00
▶	Lemon juice	NULL	$660.00
▶	Seafood	NULL	$850.00
▶	mussels	NULL	$850.00
▶ 10		$330.00	NULL
▶	Beverages	$330.00	NULL
▶	Lemon juice	$330.00	NULL
	Sum	$330.00	$1,510.00
▶ Violet Robinson		$923.00	NULL
	Sum	$1,253.00	$1,510.00

Having just a few rows in the underlying tables, as we have here, is OK for demonstration purposes, since it results in compact screenshots. To see more meaningful figures on the worksheet though, you might insert more rows into the orderitems, orders, and products underlying tables. Once you're done with it, you can click the Refresh button on the Discoverer toolbar to see an updated worksheet.

8. Select the **File | Save** menu option of Discoverer to save the worksheet discussed here.

Drilling up and down

As the name implies, drilling down is a technique you can use to float down a drill hierarchy to see data in more detail. And drilling up is the reverse operation, which you can use to slide up a drill hierarchy to see consolidated data. But what is a drill hierarchy?

Working with drill hierarchies

A drill hierarchy represents a set of items related to each other according to the foreign key relationships in the underlying tables. If a worksheet item is associated with a drill hierarchy, you can look at that hierarchy by clicking the drill icon located at the left of the heading of the worksheet item.

Suppose you want to look at the hierarchy associated with the **Orddate** item located on our worksheet at the top axis. To do this, click the **Orddate** drill icon. As a result, you should see the menu shown in the following screeenshot:

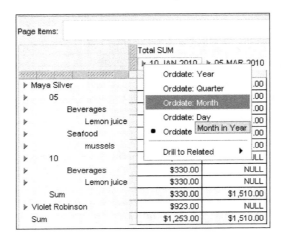

As you can see, you can drill up here from **Orddate** to **Year**, **Quarter**, or **Month**. The next screenshot illustrates what you would have if you chose **Month**.

It's important to note that you may have more than one hierarchy associated with a worksheet item. In this case, you can move on to the hierarchy you want to use through the **All Hierarchies** option on the drill menu.

Drilling down to see data in more detail

Now that you have drilled up to monthly data, can you drill down to daily figures again for a particular month? Yes, you can. Before moving any further though, let's add more data to the `orderitems` underlying table to see a more interesting layout.

Suppose you want to see more day columns under the `Jan` column. To achieve this, you need to insert items associated with an order placed by Maya Silver on any day in January but different from `10-JAN-10`, because you already have an order placed on this day. This can be done with the following statements issued from SQLPlus, assuming you're connected as `usr/usr`:

```
INSERT INTO orderitems VALUES(1003, 1111, 10, 22.0);
COMMIT;
```

Now you can refresh the data on the worksheet by clicking the **Refresh** button on the Discoverer toolbar and then click the **Jan** drill icon. In the drill menu, select **Orddate: Day**. The following screenshot illustrates what you should see as a result:

Page Items:				
	Total SUM			
	▹ Jan			▹ Mar
	▹ 10		▹ 20	
▹ Maya Silver	$330.00		$220.00	$1,510.00
▹ Beverages	$330.00		$220.00	$660.00
▹ Lemon juice	$330.00		$220.00	$660.00
▹ Seafood	NULL		NULL	$850.00
▹ mussels	NULL		NULL	$850.00
Sum	$330.00		$220.00	$1,510.00
▹ Violet Robinson	$923.00		NULL	NULL
Sum	$1,253.00		$220.00	$1,510.00

The previous example illustrates that you can drill down from a selective item, while the others presented at the same level remain collapsed. In this particular example, you drill down from the **Jan** item, while the **Mar** is still summarized.

Later, you can always collapse an expanded item by selecting the **Collapse** command in the drill menu. In this way, for example, you can collapse the **Jan** item drilled down to daily data as discussed in this section.

Drilling up to summarize data at a higher level

You've seen now how you can drill down to see the data of interest in more detail. In practice, though, you may also need to take a generalized look at your data.

Turning back to our example, let's now try to drill up from monthly data to quarter data, thus consolidating the worksheet figures. To accomplish this, you can use either the **Drill** dialog or drill menu:

1. To open the drill menu associated with the **Jan** item, click its drill icon. The menu should look like this:

   To drill up to quarter data, you can click the **Oradate: Quarter** command on the previous menu.

2. The same can be done through the **Drill** dialog, which you can open by clicking the **Drill...** command in the pop-up menu associated with each item on the worksheet. For example, if you right-click the **Jan** item and then select **Drill...** in the pop-up menu, you get to the following dialog:

As you can see, in the **Drill** dialog, unlike the drill menu, you can see where a drill-down operation is and where a drill-up one is. You can easily recognize this by the arrow next to the item to drill to. Thus, the down arrow indicates a drill-down operation and the up arrow is used to indicate a drill-up operation.

Regardless of the way you've chosen to perform the drill-up operation discussed here, the resulting worksheet should look like the following one:

So, after the drill-up operation discussed in this section, the worksheet now shows the data aggregated at the Quarter level.

Drilling from a graph

It's interesting to note that Discoverer enables you to drill from the graph associated with a worksheet. Continuing with the example in the preceding section, the graph associated with the worksheet you can see in the previous figure should look like this:

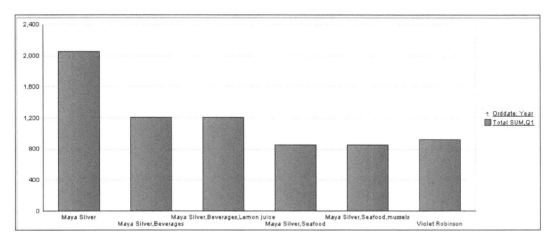

Looking to the right in the above graph, you may notice the **Orddate: Year** link, which you can click if you want to drill up to year figures. But how can you drill down to, say, month figures? The answer is you can double-click any graph bar to drill one step down. Thus, in this particular example, if you double-click a graph bar, you'll launch a drill-down from quarter data to monthly data. So the result worksheet would look like the following one:

Page Items:			
		Total SUM	
		▹ Jan	▹ Mar
▹ Maya Silver		$550.00	$1,510.00
▹	Beverages	$550.00	$660.00
▹	Lemon juice	$550.00	$660.00
▹	Seafood	NULL	$850.00
▹	mussels	NULL	$850.00
	Sum	$550.00	$1,510.00
▹ Violet Robinson		$923.00	NULL
	Sum	$1,473.00	$1,510.00

The graph will also be automatically redrawn. This should look now like the following screenshot:

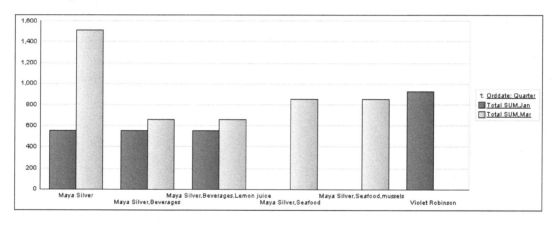

Each bar in the above graph represents figures associated with a particular month. In this particular example, this can be either January or March figures. To find out which month a given bar belongs to, you can move the mouse cursor to it and then read the information in the pop-up label. For example, if you move the cursor to the first (far left) bar, you should see the following pop-up label:

Series: Total SUM,Jan
Group: Maya Silver
Value: 550.0

As you can see from the label, the associated bar represents a January figure. So, you can double-click this bar to drill down to January daily figures. So, the worksheet should now look like this:

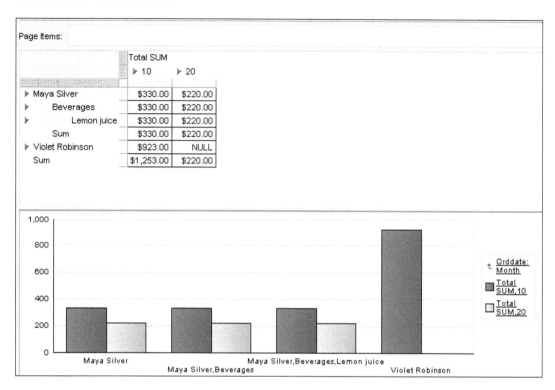

Now if you want to come back to the monthly figures, you can click the **Orddate: Day** drill icon on the top axis and select **Orddate: Month**. Moreover, if you want to see a month's figures divided into daily figures (the view you had before drilling up to quarters), you can click the drill icon next to the month of interest and select **Orddate: Day** in the menu.

Using the page items area

Often you need to select for display only part of the data you have on the worksheet. This is where the page items area above the crosstab comes in handy.

Proceeding to the example discussed here, suppose you want to select data by month, choosing a month in the items area select box. To do this, you can drag the **month** item from the top axis to the page items area. The following is the worksheet you should see as a result:

The layout will change, of course, if you select another month from the **Page Items** area select box. It's interesting to note that you're not limited to a single item to be set in the **Page Items** area. For example, you might drag the **Salesperson Name** item from the left axis. That would allow you to put another filter on the data to be displayed on the worksheet.

Summary

As you learned in this chapter, drilling is another useful tool when it comes to organizing data for more effective analysis and discovering hidden details. As you found out, Oracle Discoverer provides a set of useful drilling tools, making the task of getting answers to your business questions a breeze.

Walking through the chapter examples, you learned how to navigate through a drill hierarchy up and down, getting to the level of detail you need. You also saw how to drill to a related item, to see the detailed information for a certain item, and how to do drilling from a worksheet graph.

8
Advanced Analysis and Reporting

In this last chapter, you'll look at some advanced features of Oracle Discoverer, which you may need to answer typical business questions. The chapter begins with a discussion on how to use Discoverer parameters, workbook items that allow you to enter dynamic input values for analysis purposes. Then it proceeds to conditional formatting, explaining how you can choose what data to display on worksheets with the help of conditional formats. Finally, the chapter shows you how to make worksheet data easier to analyze with sorting.

Listed as short bullets, here are the main topics discussed in this chapter:

- Customizing worksheets to match your needs
- Analyzing worksheet data using dynamic input values
- Filtering worksheet data using conditions
- Sorting data on a worksheet

Using parameters in Discoverer

You can assign parameters to a workbook to be able then to analyze worksheet data using dynamic input values. In *Chapter 4*, *Analyzing Data and Creating Reports*, you already saw how you might take advantage of parameters, exploring an example of selecting a region's data by dynamic input. The following sections provide a more detailed look at Discoverer parameters, explaining them by example.

Analyzing worksheets by entering dynamic input values

As mentioned, the idea behind parameters is that you can enter dynamic input values to analyze worksheet data. The most common use of parameters is to allow users to specify values for filters. Going back to our example, suppose you want to analyze monthly data, displaying it for a certain month on the worksheet. The following steps will walk you through the process of creating a month parameter:

1. In the Discoverer Plus menu, choose **Tools | Parameters...** to launch the **Edit Worksheet** dialog at the **Parameters** tab.

2. On the **Parameters** tab of the **Edit Worksheet** dialog, click the **New...** button to open the **New Parameter** dialog shown in the following screenshot:

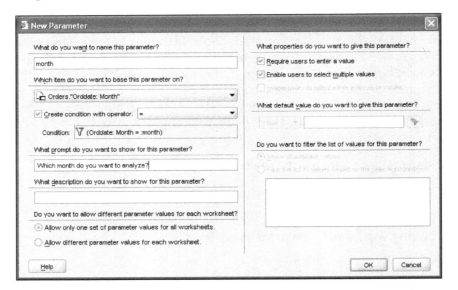

3. In the New **Parameter** dialog, enter **month** in the **What do you want to name this parameter?** edit box.

4. In the **New Parameter** dialog, select **Orders."Orddate: Month"** in the **Which item do you want to base this parameter on?** list.

5. In the New **Parameter** dialog, make sure that the **Create condition with operator:** checkbox is set and the operator in the list on the right is **=**.

6. In the **New Parameter** dialog, enter **Which month do you want to analyze?** in the **What prompt do you want to show for this parameter?** edit box.

7. In the **New Parameter** dialog, leave the other settings at their defaults and click **OK** to come back to the **Parameters** tab of the **Edit Worksheet** dialog.

8. On the **Parameters** tab of the **Edit Worksheet** dialog, in the **Available parameters** box you should see the **month** entry, as you can see it in the following screenshot:

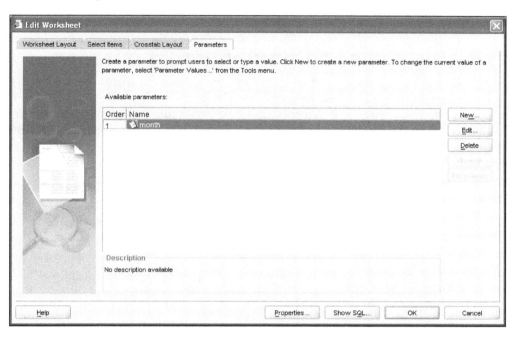

9. In the **Edit Worksheet** dialog, click **OK** to complete the creation of the parameter and come back to the worksheet.

10. Before the worksheet is displayed, the **Edit Parameter Values** dialog shown next will be displayed, prompting you to enter the month ID:

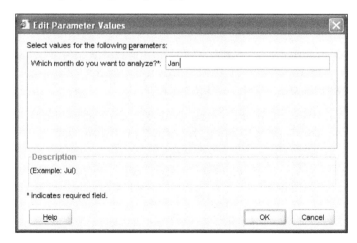

11. You can enter, for example, **Jan**, and click **OK**. As a result, you will see the worksheet containing only January figures.

12. To save the parameter, so that it persists the current session, select the **File** | **Save** menu option of Discoverer.

Changing the condition behind a parameter

If you recall from the preceding steps, you kept the **Create condition with operator** checkbox marked in the **New Parameter** dialog, with the = sign selected. This means that Discoverer implicitly created a condition. To make sure it did so, check out the **Conditions** tab in the Item Navigator. The screen you should see as the result should look like the following screenshot:

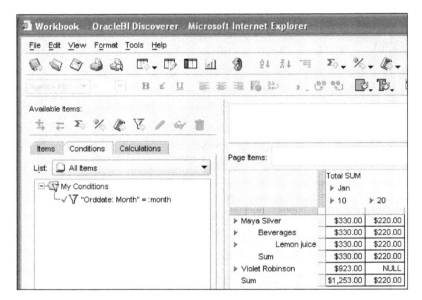

So you can always change the condition behind the parameter. For example, you may want the worksheet to display the figures for months following the one the user specifies upon opening or refreshing the worksheet. This can be done as follows:

1. On the **Conditions** tab of the Item Navigator, double-click the **"Orddate: Month"** = **:month** item to open the **Edit Condition** dialog.

2. In the **Edit Condition** dialog, click the **Condition** drop-down list in the **Formula** group and select the **>** sign from the list, as shown in the following screenshot:

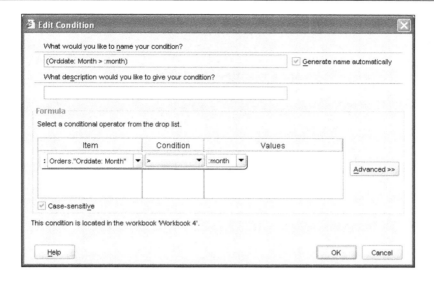

Looking through the list of available conditions, you may notice that it enables you to choose from a full spectrum of operators, including IN, IS NULL, LIKE, and BETWEEN. In the next section, you'll look at how you might use the BETWEEN operator in a condition.

3. Close the **Edit Condition** dialog by clicking **OK**.

The data on the worksheet should change immediately after closing the **Edit Condition** dialog with **OK**. The figures should now reflect the sales of the months following January, that is, all the other months except January. In this particular example though, this should be only March figures, since we've entered data for January and March only.

Filtering a worksheet with parameters

In the previous example, you've used simple operators, such as = and > in the condition associated with the month parameter. This section illustrates an example of slightly more advanced filtering. In particular, you'll see how you might take advantage of the BETWEEN operator allowing you to define a range of months whose figures you want to be displayed on the worksheet, thus specifying two parameters. To see it in action, follow these steps:

1. On the **Conditions** tab of the Item Navigator, double-click the **"Orddate: Month"** = :month item to open the **Edit Condition** dialog.

2. In the **Edit Condition** dialog, click the **Condition** checkbox in the **Formula** group and select the **BETWEEN** operator from the list.

3. In the **Edit Condition** dialog, extend the right **Values** checkbox, and choose **New Parameter...** as shown in the following screenshot:

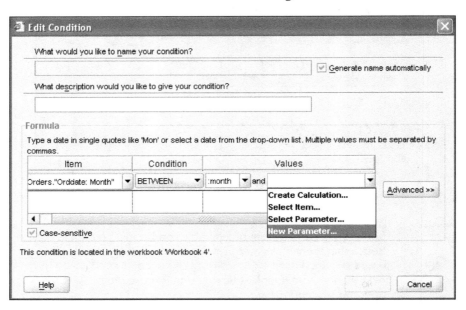

4. Once you choose **New Parameter...** in the **Values** select box, the **New Parameter** dialog should appear. In this dialog, type in the fields, creating the **end_month** parameter as shown in the following screenshot:

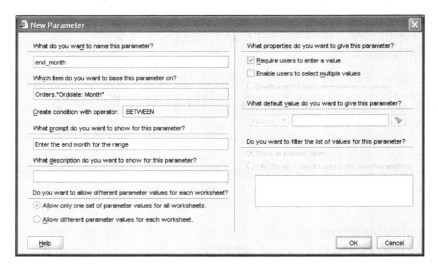

Click **OK** to come back to the **Edit Condition** dialog.

5. In the **Edit Condition** dialog, click **OK**. As a result, the **Edit Parameter Values** dialog should appear. As you can see in the following screenshot, it now asks you to enter two parameters:

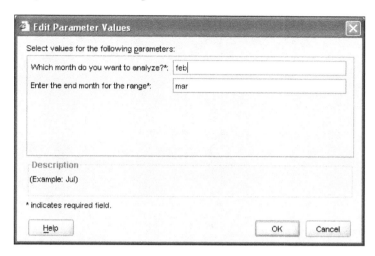

6. Suppose you enter **feb** for the first parameter value and **mar** for the second. So the worksheet being displayed should contain only March figures because there are no February figures in this example.

Conditional formatting

When you deal with a lot of data on your worksheet, it's always a good idea to highlight some data to make the entire worksheet more readable. For example, you might want to highlight all the items on the worksheet whose values are greater than 500. The following steps illustrate how you might do that:

1. Select the worksheet cells you want to format and then right-click on the selection:

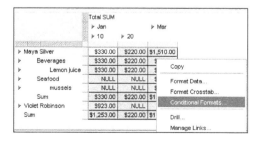

2. In the pop-up menu, select **Conditional Formats...** to open the **Conditional Formats** dialog:

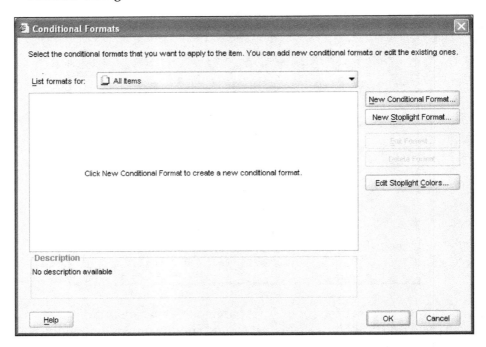

3. In the **Conditional Formats** dialog, click the **New Conditional Format...** button to open the **New Conditional Format** dialog.

4. In the **New Conditional Format** dialog, select:

    ○   **Total SUM** as the item;

    ○   **>=** as the condition;

    Then, enter **500** in the far right **Value** drop-down list, so that the dialog looks like the one shown next:

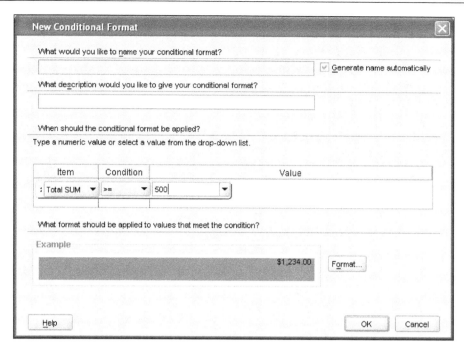

Click OK to create the conditional format and return to the **Conditional Formats** dialog.

5. In the **Conditional Formats** dialog, click **OK** to close it.

Once you've completed the above steps, you should see that the worksheet formatting has changed as follows:

| | Total SUM | | |
| | ▷ Jan | | ▷ Mar |
	▷ 10	▷ 20	
▷ Maya Silver	$330.00	$220.00	$1,510.00
▷ Beverages	$330.00	$220.00	$660.00
▷ Lemon juice	$330.00	$220.00	$660.00
▷ Seafood	NULL	NULL	$850.00
▷ mussels	NULL	NULL	$850.00
Sum	$330.00	$220.00	$1,510.00
▷ Violet Robinson	$923.00	NULL	NULL
Sum	$1,253.00	$220.00	$1,510.00

Stoplight formatting, also known as traffic-light formatting, is another interesting approach you can use to make your reports more readable. Stoplight formatting allows you to color in numeric values as unacceptable, acceptable, and desirable.

Making data easier to analyze with sorting

Sometimes you may want to change the order in which the worksheet data is sorted. In Discoverer, this can be easily done with the sorting feature. Turning back to our example, suppose you want to sort the days' figures within January from low to high. The following steps will tell you how you might do it:

1. On the worksheet and right-click the **Day** item located at the top axis.

2. In the pop-up menu, select **Sort High to Low**:

As a result, the data on the worksheet will be rearranged as follows:

Summary

In this chapter, you looked at some advanced features you can employ as a Discoverer user. In particular, you learned about parameters, conditional formatting, and sorting. As you might guess, the examples provided in the chapter were simple, just to give you a look at what is available.

Index

L

Lightweight Directory Access Protocol
   (LDAP) database 10

M

mapping, Oracle Warehouse Builder
   creating, for loading data into dimensions
      129
multidimensional data 22
multidimensional data analysis, analytic
      SQL function
   about 50
   GROUP BY … ROLLUP clause 53
   new database schema, creating 50, 51
   orders table 51, 52
multidimensional data sources
   data organization 100

N

Name field 130
new... button 86
New Conditional Format... button 164
Next button 4, 35, 40, 73

O

Online Analytical Processing (OLAP) 25
OracleAS Reports Services - Servlet
      Command Help 93
Oracle Business Intelligence
   about 25
   Business Intelligence system, backed by
      Oracle database 30
   Business Intelligence system, composing
      27-30
   Business Intelligence system, example 28
   components, list 26
   composition 26
   installing 31
   installing, process 34-39
   issues, solving 26
   Oracle Business Intelligence suite 31, 32
   Portal, Forms, Reports and Discoverer suite
      32, 33
   post-installation tasks 43-48

software, downloading 33, 34
software, requisites 31-33
tools package 26, 27
tools package, installing 41-43
Oracle Business Intelligence, components
   Oracle Discoverer Plus OLAP 26
   Oracle Discoverer Plus Relational 26
   Oracle Discoverer Portlet Provider 26
   Oracle Discoverer Viewer 26
   Oracle Reports 26
Oracle Business Intelligence, tools package
   Oracle Discoverer Administrator 26
   Oracle Discoverer Desktop 27
   Oracle Reports Developer 27
   Oracle Spreadsheet Add-In 27
   Oracle Warehouse Builder 26
Oracle Business Intelligence suite
   components 31, 32
   installing, on Windows 34-41
Oracle Business Intelligence tools package
   installing, steps 41-43
Oracle Discoverer Administrator 26
Oracle Discoverer Desktop 27
Oracle Discoverer Plus OLAP 26
Oracle Discoverer Plus Relational 26
Oracle Discoverer Portlet Provider 26
Oracle Discoverer Viewer 26
Oracle Documentation page
   URL 34
Oracle Fusion Middleware 11gR1 Software
      Downloads page
   URL 34
Oracle Reports
   about 26, 29, 91
   building, with Reports Builder 93-98
   Reports Server, starting up 91-93
Oracle Reports Developer 27
Oracle Spreadsheet Add-In 27
Oracle Warehouse Builder
   about 26, 100
   cube, creating 120, 121
   cube mapping, creating 130, 131
   database objects, importing 112-115
   deploying 131
   Design Center, launching 108, 109
   dimensional data stores, building 108
   dimensions, creating 117

staging mapping, Oracle Warehouse Builder
  creating 122-127
staging table, Oracle Warehouse Builder
  building 121, 122
  with data, loading 128, 129
SUM aggregate function 64, 80

T

target structures, Oracle Warehouse Builder
  defining 115
  dimensions, creating 117
  Product dimension, creating 119, 120
  Region dimension, creating 120
  target module, creating 115-117
  Time dimension, creating 117-119
Time dimension, Oracle Warehouse Builder
  creating 117-119
transactional database
  reporting against 21

U

UNITPRICE attribute 127
User Name and Password fields 48
Users node 115

V

VALUE attribute 127
Viewer, Discoverer 29, 89, 90

W

Warehouse Builder repository schema
  creating 103, 104
Warehouse Builder workspace
  creating 104-108
warehouses 99
windowing function, analytic SQL function
  about 60
  AVG function 61
  ROWS BETWEEN clause 61
  sliding_avg field 61
Windows-only applications 34
workbooks 17
worksheet items
  calculation, creating 138, 139
  drag and drop feature, used for pivoting 142, 143
  pivoting 138
  worksheet layout, changing 139-142
worksheet layout, worksheet items
  changing 139-142
worksheets
  analyzing, by entering dynamic input values 158-160
  filtering, with parameters 161-163

X

X button 139
XQuery 61

Thank you for buying
Oracle Business Intelligence: The Condensed Guide to Analysis and Reporting

About Packt Publishing

Packt, pronounced 'packed', published its first book "Mastering phpMyAdmin for Effective MySQL Management" in April 2004 and subsequently continued to specialize in publishing highly focused books on specific technologies and solutions.

Our books and publications share the experiences of your fellow IT professionals in adapting and customizing today's systems, applications, and frameworks. Our solution based books give you the knowledge and power to customize the software and technologies you're using to get the job done. Packt books are more specific and less general than the IT books you have seen in the past. Our unique business model allows us to bring you more focused information, giving you more of what you need to know, and less of what you don't.

Packt is a modern, yet unique publishing company, which focuses on producing quality, cutting-edge books for communities of developers, administrators, and newbies alike. For more information, please visit our website: www.packtpub.com.

About Packt Enterprise

In 2010, Packt launched two new brands, Packt Enterprise and Packt Open Source, in order to continue its focus on specialization. This book is part of the Packt Enterprise brand, home to books published on enterprise software – software created by major vendors, including (but not limited to) IBM, Microsoft and Oracle, often for use in other corporations. Its titles will offer information relevant to a range of users of this software, including administrators, developers, architects, and end users.

Writing for Packt

We welcome all inquiries from people who are interested in authoring. Book proposals should be sent to author@packtpub.com. If your book idea is still at an early stage and you would like to discuss it first before writing a formal book proposal, contact us; one of our commissioning editors will get in touch with you.

We're not just looking for published authors; if you have strong technical skills but no writing experience, our experienced editors can help you develop a writing career, or simply get some additional reward for your expertise.

Oracle Warehouse Builder 11g: Getting Started

ISBN: 978-1-847195-74-6   Paperback: 368 pages

Extract, Transform, and Load data to build a dynamic, operational data warehouse

1. Build a working data warehouse from scratch with Oracle Warehouse Builder

2. Cover techniques in Extracting, Transforming, and Loading data into your data warehouse

3. Learn about the design of a data warehouse by using a multi-dimensional design with an underlying relational star schema

Mastering Oracle Scheduler in Oracle 11g Databases

ISBN: 978-1-847195-98-2   Paperback: 240 pages

Schedule, manage, and execute jobs that automate your business processes

1. Automate jobs from within the Oracle database with the built-in Scheduler

2. Boost database performance by managing, monitoring, and controlling jobs more effectively

3. Contains easy-to-understand explanations, simple examples, debugging tips, and real-life scenarios

Please check **www.PacktPub.com** for information on our titles

www.ingramcontent.com/pod-product-compliance
Lightning Source LLC
La Vergne TN
LVHW062317060326
832902LV00013B/2272